MW00559347

Mei Ying Sheng performing Single Whip

TAI CHI TRAINING IN CHINA

Howard Thomas

Paul H. Crompton Ltd.
94 Felsham Road
London SW15 1DQ
England

First Edition 1997

ISBN No 1-874250-70-7

London: Paul H. Crompton Ltd.
94 Felsham Road, London SW15 1DQ, England

New York: Talman Company
131 Spring Street, New York, N.Y. 10012, U.S.A.

Printed and bound in England

by Caric Press

Clerwood, Corunna Main,

Andover, Hants SP10 1JE

(01264) 354887

CONTENTS

Introduction

1. *Yi Lu Shun Feng* : Have a Nice Trip 3
2. *Hu Tou She Wei* : Tiger's Head Snake's Tail 13
3. Getting Out and Getting Back 32
4. The Shenyang Institute of Physical Culture 42
5. *Yi Jian Shuang Diao* : One Arrow Two Targets 66
6. What's in a Name? Teacher, Coach or Master 85
7. Tai Chi as a Sport or an Art : Fish or Bear's Paw 96
8. Flavour : A Taste of China 107
9. Softness Within Hardness, Hardness Within Softness . 117
10. Language as the Key to Culture 128
11. Looking for the Master Within Oneself 134

Conclusion 137

INTRODUCTION

According to Lao Zi :*"Qian Li Zhi Xing, Shi Yu Zu Xia"* (千里之行， 始于足下). There are thousands of idioms, maxims and sayings in Chinese. This is just one of them and there are many more scattered throughout the pages of this book. It means literally a journey of a thousand miles starts from the bottom of your foot. However great the venture, enterprise or undertaking may be, it still has a small beginning. The first step is the most significant. I took one step in March 1989 which turned into an epic journey of five years spent living, working, studying and marrying in China. One day I plan to return to live there and I shall probably die there, such is the great fondness and affinity that I have developed with the country, its people and its culture.

"Bai Wen Bu Ru Yi Jian" (百闻不如一见) means a hundred times hearing about something cannot be compared with once seeing something in person. Many people dream of going to study martial arts in China. Some realize that dream and spend a couple of weeks in Beijing. Some even spend three or four months training with a teacher or traditional master. However, I doubt that few if any will have spent such a prolonged period in China as myself. I even suffered culture shock on my eventual return to England in August 1994, so deeply was I rooted in the Chinese way. I wasn't by any means a young man when I went. I was actually forty years old. Some might say that I was suffering from the mid-life crisis. I would certainly agree that I was at a crossroads in my life and going nowhere in particular. Taking that first step was the turning point in my life. I wish that I had taken it earlier but, as with so many other aspects of my time in China, fate seemed to play a critical part in the timing. I was destined to go when I did, destined to live in the places I did, destined to study with my particular teachers, destined to meet my future wife and destined still for I know not what exactly in the future. Whatever that destiny may hold, I am satisfied with what I have already achieved and am delighted to have been given the opportunity to share my experiences. I have realized my dream. If I can in some small way inspire others to follow in my footsteps or strike out on their own path, my satisfaction would be even greater.

This book is the first in a trilogy dedicated to a description of my life in China through the eyes and perspective not only of a foreigner but of a tai chi student and teacher in particular. It is one person's individual account of learning tai chi on a day to day basis. It aims to be honest, practical, accessible and demystifying. It does not aim to tell the definitive story. I can only describe what happened to me. Someone else's story may be totally different. That is the beauty of China. It is such a vast, unpredictable country where absolutely anything may happen and often does.

What were my aims? And to what extent were these aims realized? To be honest,

I didn't really have any fixed targets. I just wanted to go to China to study tai chi. Exactly what I would find there was in the lap of the gods. I had no set intinerary or schedule. I simply allowed myself to be swept along with the tide of events which overtook the country in the late eighties and early nineties. I could not have known at that time what turbulent and historic events would envelop me. I became deeply emotionally and psychologically embroiled in the run-up to and aftermath of the Tian An Men Square turmoil. My tai chi training became inextricably caught up in these events. I was forced to examine myself, my art, and my soul. Any aims which I might have had at the outset became purely academic and peripheral as I was compelled to focus on the core values of my life and my very existence. For a while I even doubted that tai chi had any significant role to play at all. Eventually, however, in such extreme times I found solace, tranquillity, strength and even sanity in the art of tai chi in a world which had temporarily lost its equibilirium. *Dong Zhong Qiu Jing* （动中求静）- In the midst of movement, seek calm.

YI LU SHUN FENG
(我在中国)
Have a Nice Trip!

It was midnight on Wednesday, the 29th of March 1989 as PIA flight 218 soared high above Iran. The city of Tehran sprawled below, its lights glistening like the sequins on a black cloak. Most of the passengers were sleeping peacefully or dozing in the semi-darkness. I alone was wide awake, too excited to sleep. It was the dawn of a great adventure for me. I was on my way to China.

At that moment the captain announced over the intercom that we were going to encounter some rather nasty turbulence and that all passengers should fasten their safety belts. No sooner had he finished speaking than the plane was being severely buffeted by strong winds and we suddenly lost altitude. Everyone screamed with fear as their hearts leapt into their mouths. People clung to their seats and to each other as panic broke out. The stewards rushed to try and restore calm. Instead they were hurled uncontrollably down the gangway as once more we fell from the sky. This time there was no screaming, only a communal sharp intake of breath. Thoughts raced through the mind. What was I doing on this plane anyway? Why hadn't I stayed safely at home in England with my feet firmly on the ground? What were my motives for going to China? Would I ever live to tell the tale? At the centre of all the chaos around me I felt very calm and composed as though in the eye of a storm. If the plane did go down now, and this really was the end, I felt happy and at peace with my decision. Deciding to go to China was the turning point in my life. If the new road turned out to be a short one, then so be it but I was convinced it was the right road. The question was how did I come to be sitting in seat H5 on this 747 in the first place.

It all went back to nine years earlier. In 1980 I had watched a series of programmes on BBC2 about the Yorkshire Dance Centre in Leeds and the kind of movement classes it offered, from classical ballet to jazz dance to tai chi. Tai chi - that looked and sounded fascinating. I went along to a class and enrolled. The teacher was Christina Bunney who was a student of Gerda Geddes - the lady principally instrumental for introducing tai chi into Britain. From the first moment, I was hooked. I could not really explain its attraction - a certain indefinable quality , engendering a peaceful serenity, and harmony of mind and body. Whatever its allure, it held my interest for the next seven or eight years. During this time, I graduated from student to assistant to substitute teacher whenever Christina was pregnant, which seemed to happen on a fairly regular basis. I also set up my own classes in and around my home town of Barnsley in Yorkshire. I taught adult education classes, in colleges and universities, at hospitals and sports clubs. My students came from many different backgrounds and were drawn to tai chi for a myriad different reasons.They came from martial arts, yoga, athletics, dance, music, medicine and mental health. Gradually the scope of my classes grew so much that it ended up as a full time occupation. By 1988 I was, however, beginning to grow restless. I felt that I had taken my tai chi as far as I could in England. I needed to learn more. I needed to get to the source. In short, I needed to go to China.

Of course, many people talk about doing such a thing. Few people if any actually realize their dreams. In the end, I spent nearly five years in China, returning for good to the West in August 1994. The problem was how to get there in the first place. While thumbing through the local phone book, I found the number and address of the China Services Centre based in Sheffield. This organisation had its roots in the strong civic links established by the County of South Yorkshire with the Province of Liaoning in China's industrial North-East which had a similar preponderance of heavy industry, steel and coal. It offered expert advice and assistance with the development of bilateral business and cultural exchanges. I went along and had a friendly chat with the director. He was extremely positive and full of encouragement without being able to give me any actual concrete help. However, he did give me the name and address of a Chinese professor on sabbatical at Sheffield University. He was Yang En Tang, Professor of English from Qingdao University in Shandong Province. I had already heard of Qingdao as it was famous for producing reputedly the finest beer in China. The professor's name also rang a bell with me but I didn't know where from. I went home and wrote a letter to Professor Yang, informing him of my proposal and asking for his advice. On the bookshelf above my writing desk, my eyes landed on one of the many books I had bought over the years on the subject of Chinese internal arts including tai chi. This was a book entitled Chinese Qigong Therapy written and published in China by the Shandong Science and Technology Press in 1985. This book written originally in Chinese by Zhang Ming Wu and Sun Xing Yuan had been translated into English by none other than my friend to be Yang En Tang and his wife Yao Xiu Qing.

On receipt of my letter, Professor Yang invited me to his house in Sheffield which he shared with three other visiting professors. We quickly became firm friends and he vowed to give me as much assistance as he could. The best avenue open to me seemed to be to travel to China on a student visa and enrol on a Chinese language course. In my spare time, I could pursue my interests in Chinese internal arts. Through his contacts at the People's University in Jinan, the capital city of Shandong Province, Professor Yang arranged for me to enrol as an overseas student. It wasn't exactly what I was hoping for and I would have to find an outlay of several thousand US dollars to cover the costs of my studies. Not wishing to appear ungrateful, I initially agreed to go along with this course of action, providing nothing else cropped up. In the event, something did crop up, and from a most unlikely source.

Reading my local weekly paper, the Barnsley Chronicle, one Friday morning I discovered that Barnsley had a twin town in China called Fuxin. Not only that, but by an amazing coincidence and quirk of fate, there were vacancies at that very moment for three people who would like to take part in a cultural exchange scheme between the two towns. The timing could not have been more propitious. Three burghers from the Metropolitan Borough Council of Barnsley were requested to change places with three cooks from Fuxin who would study Yorkshire cuisine at Barnsley Technical College. This proposal conjured up unlikely images of the good people of Fuxin tucking into such local delicacies as Yorkshire puddings filled with onion gravy and the famous Barnsley chops. Whilst on the other hand, the Barnsley exchangees would pass on the skills of Chinese water-colour painting and calligraphy to the miners of Barnsley Main Colliery. Or maybe not. At any rate it was a golden opportunity at which I jumped. For visa purposes I received an official invitation from my host organization - the Liaoning People's Association for Friendship with Foreign Countries. I had to pay my own plane fare but I would receive free board and lodging for three months and would even receive a small monthly salary. I was only made aware of this possibility at the eleventh hour and the director of management services at Barnsley Town Hall was of great assistance in smoothing my passage. On the eve of my departure, I asked him, "What about the other two?" to which he replied, "What other two? You're the only one going."

And so it turned out to be a unique and solitary adventure to China - more interesting and more dangerous for all that - just the way I liked it. Armed only with a modicum of broken Chinese gleaned from a BBC tape, I embarked on the most fascinating and challenging period of my life. I bade farewell or "*Zai Jian*" (再见) to England and hello or "*Ni Hao*" (你好) to China.

The plane didn't crash. Almost everyone was sick. Remarkably, for a very poor traveller, I was one of the few people who didn't succumb to nausea. I nearly did when I first saw the pea-green interior walls of Beijing Airport in all its splendour. This must be one of the the poorest international capital airports in the world - especially designed to give incoming passengers the least impressive welcome. After negotiating the customs, I picked up my rucksack and staggered out into the entrance hall, feeling as if I had set foot on an alien planet. China wasn't just the other side of the world. It felt like a completely different world altogether. I shivered with a mixture of excitement and fear - a combination of emotions that I was to feel many more times during my stay in PRC. Among the Chinese signs, I picked out one in English, "Change". I needed some Chinese money. On Professor Yang's advice, I had brought with me in my money pouch US dollars which apparently were more readily acceptable than the good old British pound. From what I had read, I also knew that China operated a dual currency system - the unit of currency being the *Yuan* (元) or *Renminbi* (人民币) - People's Currency - which was used by Chinese people and the FEC (Foreign Exchange Certificate) which was used by foreigners in China. FEC's could be used in the Friendship Stores, which were supposedly only accessible to foreigners and were the only places you could buy high quality consumer goods. I was also soon to learn that both US dollars and FEC's could be exchanged on the blackmarket for up to twice their face value in *Yuan*. Anyway, I changed 300 dollars, so giving me a total of 1085 FEC's. I felt much more comfortable now with a supply of readies in my pocket.

In China I soon discovered that it was nigh impossible to get things done as quickly as you wanted. You had to take things one step at a time and mostly this involved very small steps indeed. In China, life did not mirror art. It mirrored bureaucracy. Everything was slow, painstakingly, excruciatingly slow. And everything closed for two hours at lunch when you most wanted to get things done. This was in order to accommodate the Chinese custom of taking a midday siesta for an hour or two. Anyway, my first step had been achieved. I had some money in my pocket. The second step was to negotiate the journey between the airport and the city centre. I didn't even know how far it was. There was a distinct lack of helpful signs in English to guide me. I eventually wandered out onto the forecourt and was immediately besieged by a posse of taxi and minicab drivers who each grabbed a handful of me. I found myself being yanked in a dozen different directions at once. Chinese taxi drivers do not stand on ceremony. They tend to claim you as a prize from the clutches of other taxi drivers and transport you away to their lair like the spoils of victory. Having managed to extricate myself from this manhandling, I selected a relatively docile driver in what looked like a small fruit and vegetable van passing as a taxi.I jumped in the back and in my best Chinese said, "*Dao Tiyubinguan*" (Take me to the Sports Hotel). He smiled broadly showing me a set of rotting black teeth with chunks of green vegetable between them. I smiled back. Contact had been made. We had lift off.

We bumped and bounced along the road to the capital for about an hour. It was a long and dusty road with absolutely nothing that could be described as scenery en route and I had the added attraction of a strong smell of oil and petrol wafting all around me. My driver was quite a friendly chap and chatted merrily to me in Mandarin. I managed to smile, grunt and nod my way through the conversation, even interjecting such wonderful questions as "*Ni shi Beijingren ma*?" (Are you from Beijing?) and "*Yuan bu yuan*?" (Is it far?). I felt that I had really achieved something when I asked, "*Nin gui xing*?" (What is your name?) and he replied, "*Xing Li.*" (My name is Li). But most of what I tried to say in Chinese to Mr Li was totally unintelligible to him as I had less than a complete mastery of the subtle tones of spoken Chinese. I did manage to pick out the fact that he thought I was French, perhaps because by this time I had resorted to gesticulations to get my meaning across. Still I thought I had done extremely well on my first real verbal exchange with a native Chinese. I must have been happy as when it came to paying the fare I readily stumped up the 120 yuan he was demanding. I even gave him a 10 yuan tip. I later found out I that I could have caught the airport bus for 7 yuan, so saving me nearly twenty pounds. But I was learning.

My first impressions of Beijing were rather disappointing. It was all so new. Everything was made of concrete. The city looked grey. There was hardly a hint of the ancient capital epitomised by the Forbidden City. It was a city seemingly intent on ripping down the old and slapping up the new as fast as humanly possible. It was almost possible to see the many tall new office blocks, department stores, friendship hotels and apartment buildings rise up before your eyes as the building workers swarmed like ants over the new edificies on the intricate exterior scaffolding made up of bamboo. The main avenues were endlessly long and endlessly wide. Fortunately the streets were relatively uncongested as at that time there were few privately owned cars. This was more than made up for by the bicycle population. And most of them looked identical - Flying Pigeons or Phoenixes. I marvelled at how people were able to identify and relocate their own bikes among the massed ranks of the thousands parked by the side of the road. The locks were extremely flimsy and one key would open a thousand different bicycles. I supposed that if somebody took yours by mistake then you could simply take the next one and nobody would bother too much. And the people. The population of China was approaching 1.2 billion. The problem was that they all seemed to be here in Beijing, stopping me from getting where I wanted to go. The best policy seemed to be to go with the flow and they would eventually take you where you wanted to go.

I had purposely chosen this hotel. The *Tiyu Binguan* (Sports Hotel) was in the south of the city within walking distance of Tiantan Park, the largest park in central Beijing where I knew a lot of tai chi players practised in the morning. I booked a room for 7 nights at 90 yuan a night. I wasn't due in Fuxin until the following Thursday so would have a week to find my feet and get acclimatized. Many foreigners who arrive in China for the first time make arrangements to be met at the capital airport, to be chauffeured around in a car and to be chaperoned by an interpreter and guide. I disposed with all of the above, preferring to struggle through and get by on my own. Some people thought I must be crazy to do this. Having eventually lived in China for several years, I realize that being a little crazy is all part of the secret to survival in the Middle Kingdom. By now a warm feeling of security was beginning to replace the cold sweaty-palmed sensation of my first arrival. Buoyed by my new-found confidence I decided to take a walk and unwind . By now it was around nine o'clock and already dusk. I had hardly gone a few steps when someone said "Hello" to me. And then I heard my first "*Lao wai*" (老外) which I was to hear all over China. Chinese people say it about you rather than to you, although it is always within your earshot. It simply means foreigner or outsider. It may be just a curious observation as they haven't seen many foreigners before, or it may be spat with contempt in the sense of bloody foreigner or simply uttered as a term of endearment. The intended meaning was dependent on the delivery. I have to admit that it really got on my nerves at first but eventually I got used to it.

I found that I was the object of curious gazes from all directions and turned up the collar on my coat to appear less conspicuous. It was relatively easy to go unnoticed in the dark early evenings. There was no street lighting in large areas of Chinese towns and cities. Cyclists were not obliged to use lights. Even cars and buses did not usually bother to switch on their headlights as their drivers thought that it wore out the battery. At crossroads after a certain hour, both sets of traffic lights were programmed to flash amber simultaneously which further increased the daredevil and cavalier attitude of the drivers, cyclists and pedestrians. I witnessed many road acidents in China, some fatal and some simply amusing. I saw fights and heated arguments, all of which drew large crowds.In fact it is one of the most popular forms of entertainment in China to watch two people having a really good verbal duel or a bout of fisticuffs in the middle of the road. I once saw a cyclist knocked off his bike by a long metal tube carried by someone crossing the street. The cyclist retaliated by attacking him with a volley of steamed buns. In the wake of such incidents, a large crowd of onlookers usually gathers, sometimes completely blocking the road, so leading to increased friction, other accidents and an even greater crowd. On this particular twilight evening, people and objects loomed in and out of the darkness barely missing each other with scant regard for safety. The only source of light came from the pavements where young men played snooker on decrepit tables with torn cloths and knobbly balls. The tables were overhung with naked light bulbs which the players had enterprisingly hooked up to the overhead power lines. I continued to walk around the perimeter of Tian Tan Park, peering through the windows of small family restaurants and corner shops at the food and goods on display. Everything was so fascinating. I kept on walking until I decided I had had enough and turned around to head back for the hotel. Strangely everything looked different approaching from the opposite direction. My newly-found confidence slowly began to ebb away, to be replaced with an empty feeling of uncertainty. There seemed fewer people now. The pavements were less brightly lit. All the snooker players had disappeared. I could not pick out a single landmark. Slowly it dawned on me. I was lost. How could it have happened? I had only walked around the block, following the outer perimeter of the park. There was a junction ahead. If I turned right, opposite the entrance to the park that should be my street with the Sports Hotel on the right. But it was not there. I started to panic. Why had I been so stupid as to leave the warm security of my hotel? I was tired, sick and jet lagged after an 18 hour flight. What on earth had possessed me to saunter around a strange city at night?

Two old men were approaching. I rushed up to them and asked, "*Tiyubinguan zai nar?*" (Where is the Sports Hotel?) They looked at each other then looked back at me. Obviously they had not understood. My tones were not right. Was *Ti* second tone or third tone? Was *Yu* fourth tone or first tone? My basic Chinese began to disintegrate rapidly as I tried to permutate all the possible tones. "*Tiyubinguan zai nar?*" I repeated. The two old men simply shook their heads, laughed and walked on muttering, "*Lao wai*". I spotted a security guard smoking at the entrance to a block of flats. I started to run towards it. He saw me coming and responded by jumping inside his cosy box, locking the door behind him. I tapped on the window frantically. I must have presented a frightening picture to him. What on earth did the crazy foreigner want? He was not going to open up and find out for all the tea in China. He turned his back and puffed deliberately on his cigarette. From there I started to run.I do not remember in which direction. I just ran. I do not know for how long - five minutes or fifteen minutes in all directions until suddenly I spotted it. I arrived at the junction and there it was - the neon light announcing the presence of the *Tiyubinguan*. It was now around half past eleven, two and a half hours since I had set out. Hot, sweaty and red in the face I burst through the doors into the lobby. There was no one about except for the night receptionist. She fixed me with a startled gaze. As coolly as I could, I simply said, 'I've just been out for a walk," dashed to the lift, went up to my room, collapsed on my bed and slept till ten the next morning.

Needless to say, for the next few days I kept a low profile. I asked at hotel reception where I should buy a train ticket to Fuxin. They had never heard of the place but recommended that I should go to the Beizhan, Bejing's central railway station. I spent some time buying tai chi books at the Foreign Language Bookstore on *Wang Fu Jing*, the main shopping street in Beijing, and took in a few of the tourist sights. I hooked up with a young Swedish guy staying at the hotel. His name was Pol Tom Polsen. He had been in the States for five years studying agriculture in North Dakota and was doing the Far East on his way home. We did the Great Wall, bought the badge and the T shirt and then the Ming Tombs, no badge and no T-shirt. After that it was on to Mao Ze Dong's Mausoleum, where we filed past the very pink body of the late Chairman. At least it was free. Finally on to the Forbidden City which was an extortionate twelve *yuan* for foreigners (Nowadays, it's 50 *yuan* or more) . I really resented the two-tier pricing system in China. There was one price for the Chinese and another price for the so-called foreign guests. They seemed to think that all foreign tourists were rich. I wanted to point out to them that I was not German or Japanese but a poor English tai chi teacher, to whom they should be grateful for promoting one of their national treasures and on whom they should really take pity and let into these sights for nothing.There was even a special price for foreigners to get into the parks! That night I heard on the 10 o'clock CCTV news in English that a man had been arrested for stealing 55 relics and treasures from the Ming Tombs in Shenyang, Liaoning Province. After a brief trial he could look forward to a swift and summary execution. The family of the condemned man even had to buy the bullets which the firing squad used to carry out the execution. They don't mess around with the justice system in China.

Tom suggested that if I wanted to buy a train ticket, I should go to the CITS office (China International Travel Service) in the Qongwenmen Hotel where he had stayed on a previous visit. They had not heard of Fuxin either and told me to go to the International Passengers Booking Office in the main concourse at Beijing Central railway station. *Beijing Huochezhan* (Beijing Railway Station) more commonly known as *Beizhan*, is surely one of the major tourist attractions of Beijing - much more interesting than the Great Wall and the Forbidden City. And it was free!

Buying any kind of ticket in China is a nightmare. The best way is to get one of your Chinese friends whose first cousin three times removed works in the ticket office to get you one through the back door or *Hou Men*. This system is endemic in Chinese society and culture. It even has a name - *Guanxi* (关系) which literally means connection or relationship. We might regard it as corruption but the Chinese would take a much more pragmatic approach. It is simply an easier way of getting things done. Of course, you could alternatively buy a ticket on the black market. But unless you are familiar with the Chinese inscriptions on the ticket, this is not advisable as you may end up shelling out for an out of date hard seat ticket to Shanghai when you wanted a soft sleeper ticket to Chengdu. Or it may even be a complete fake. Even the real tickets look like fakes! Anyway at least in Beijing there is a special facility for foreigners who wish to buy train tickets. In some of the out of way places you just have to queue up with the locals for hours, only to be told when you reach the front of the queue that you are at the wrong window and you have to join the back of another queue to wait for another few hours. But the sense of triumph and elation when you succeed in buying a ticket in China can only be equalled by winning an Olympic gold medal, such are the lengths of dedication, endurance and sheer bloody-mindedness required.

Beijing station has a massive forecourt on which you will find thousands of travellers eating, drinking, sleeping , living and maybe even some dying; but all of them waiting. The cheapest and most convenient way of travelling around China is by train.Taking internal flights in China can seriously damage your health as their safety record is not exactly one hundred per cent. The train is the best way to get to know

China and the Chinese people. My longest journey was about 36 hours hard seat from Shenzhen to Shanghai.(I flew back!) After passing through the main entrance of Beijing station, I made my way to the left of the escalator to the rear of the concourse where I found the swing doors announcing "International Passengers Booking Office". Inside was a vast waiting area with row upon row of plastic seats occupied by travellers who seemed to age visibly before my eyes as they waited interminably for the announcement of their trains. In the top left hand corner was the ticket office. Here backpackers from all over the world were buying tickets to all the far-flung corners of China. As this was my first visit, I hadn't got a clue what to do. Fortunately, in the face of a distinct lack of helpfulness on the Chinese part, most foreigners were only too pleased to help out their fellow travellers. I was told to look for my destination on the huge timetables in Chinese and English on the wall, then fill in a reservation form, take it to window one, get a confirmation slip then go to either window two or three to pay for my ticket in FEC's.

I needed to arrive in Fuxin the following Friday morning so I would have to catch the Thursday night train. Now Fuxin is only a small place and so far no one had even heard of it. I knew that it lay on the line to Shenyang which is the largest city in the northeast of China. On the timetable I found a train leaving around ten p.m. and filled in the form with the relevant details. When I eventually got to the front of the queue, I realised that none of the counter clerks spoke English. This was the International Passengers Booking Office but nobody here spoke any foreign languages. This was typically, paradoxically Chinese. I grew to love such paradoxes but right now I was frustrated. Still, I had the ideal opportunity to practise my Chinese. The clerk shook her head and asked, "*Dao nali qu*?" (Where are you going?) I replied, "Fuxin." She shook her head again. I began to fear that this town didn't even exist and that I had travelled half way around the world to a mythical Chinese destination. She prodded her finger at the form "*Shenyang bu xing*" (Shenyang, no good). Then she repeated slowly, "*Dan Dong*" . I looked blank. So far my basic Chinese had held out but this time I didn't understand what she was trying to tell me. "*Dan Dong*," she repeated more loudly and more impatiently as if by turning up the volume I would be able to understand. It was then that a helpful Malaysian Chinese lady from behind me in the queue caught my attention and pointed at the timetable on the wall, smiled and said, "Dan Dong, you need the Dan Dong train." Now I got it. I couldn't travel to Fuxin on the Shenyang train. I had to take the Dandong train.

I withdrew from the queue, filled in another form and rejoined the back of the queue. When I eventually got to the front of the queue again, the same clerk looked at me as if I were a complete stranger. No sense of recognition or sympathy. She simply went through the motions, stamped my form and indicated I should move over to window two. I paid my 91 yuan in FEC's and held in my hot, sweaty, little hand a soft sleeper ticket for Fuxin on Thursday the 6th April departing at 9.40 pm. What an amazing feeling of satisfaction. I punched the air in victory and shouted, "Yes." Everyone else in the ticket office knew exactly what I was feeling. Now I was really on my way!

HU TOU SHE WEI
(虎头蛇尾)
TIGER'S HEAD SNAKE'S TAIL

When I arrived in China I still wasn't sure what a master was, but presumed I would recognise one when I saw one. Initially I suffered from that disease common to all westerners who immediately equate a Chinese face with expertise in martial arts. Eventually after several years in China I became extremely difficult to impress, having witnessed the skills of masters, coaches and teachers at the very highest level.

My first contact with a teacher of any kind in China was ironically with someone called Yang in Tian Tan Park one morning during my week-long stay in Beijing on my first arrival in the capital. He was, appropriately enough for his name, teaching traditional Yang style to a group who gathered there every morning. I soon found that the fact that I was not only interested in tai chi but was also a practitioner and even a teacher opened many doors to me. The group was used to interested foreigners stopping and staring at their morning practice and even posing politely for photos with them, but they were delighted to find a foreigner who understood and shared their passion for tai chi.

Yang stopped the class and respectfully asked me to show him my form. I cringe with embarrassment when I look back now on such early encounters in China. At that time I thought my tai chi was pretty good and proceeded to run through the 108 step form. Yang and his class stood in respectful silence and clapped enthusiastically when I had finished. I realise now that their politeness and apparent appreciation was exactly that - polite appreciation. Several years later when I could justifiably maintain that my standard was quite high even by Chinese standards, these early demonstrations filled me with acute embarrassment. They asked me to return the next day and join the class. I agreed if I had the time. However, as with many similar brief encounters, it turned out to be a one-off and I never saw them again.

I had, nevertheless, learned several lessons. Firstly, that tai chi was a means of communication in itself. It immediately brought me onto the same wavelength as my Chinese hosts. Secondly, that my inability to speak and understand Chinese was a barrier to the deeper knowledge that any teacher or master might wish to impart to me. Fortunately, in these early days, there always seemed to be a middle-aged lady in these classes who just happened to be an English teacher. How long could I rely on a friendly interpreter if I eventually wanted to have a one-to-one relationship with a tai chi master? Thirdly, therefore, I had to learn Chinese. This was my biggest lesson. My last lesson was that I had to virtually forget everything that I had learned in my previous 9 years in England. Frankly, my tai chi was worthless. I eventually learned a great deal of humility in the face of the fantastic skills of my teachers. But I was still flushed with the success of being a novelty and enjoyed basking in the glow of my notoriety. I had always been quite a shy person but I suddenly found myself turning into an extrovert exhibitionist whenever the subject of tai chi came up. I hope you will pardon my temporary self indulgence. More than anything, I learned that I had a great deal to learn, which accounts for the fact that I kept on returning to China and spent nearly five years there in total. Not only that, but that I could learn something from everyone - not only teachers but also fellow students. I learned a great deal about the art of tai chi but in its pursuit I learned even more about myself. It was a totally liberating experience. Before going to China, I had lost myself. I had no real direction or meaning in my life. My pursuit of the true nature and art of tai chi was a vehicle that opened many doors within myself.

I left Beijing on the evening of Thursday the 6th of April 1989 on the Dandong train for Fuxin. I was filled with a sense of expectation , excitement and not a little fear. It was symptomatic of all my time in China that I experienced such contradictory emotions. This particular phase began in the words of the Chinese idiom : *Hu Tou She Wei* with high hopes as represented by the Tiger's Head and ended in tragedy and despair in the shape of the Snake's Tail. At his point in time I was blissfully unaware of what the future had in store.

We departed from *Beizhan* at 9.50 p.m. from platform six. The female attendant took my ticket and gave me a metal disc corresponding to my bunk in the soft sleeper compartment. I flopped into bed and fell asleep. The next thing I knew it was morning. The sun was up and so were the people - with towels and toilet bags slung over their shoulders, they were washing and brushing fiercely. I looked at my watch. It was 6.15. The attendant was bringing us flasks of boiling water for tea. I asked her, " *Ji dian dao Fuxin*?" (What time do we get to Fuxin?) "*Qi dian ban*" (Half past seven) she replied. When we arrived, the attendant gave me back my ticket and I handed over my disc. I should like to have hung on to it as a memento of my first real train journey in China. At that time, I wanted to keep everything that passed through my hands as a momento.

I was met at Fuxin railway station by a delegation from the City Foreign Affairs Office. They whisked me off in a smart black car to the Xi Shan Hotel - the number one place in town. At seven o'clock that evening, they returned and took me to a private dining hall for a banquet with the Mayor, the Director of the Foreign Affairs Office and various other local dignitaries. From the very first moment, I was treated as a VIP. If I had been the Prime Minister of Great Britain, I could not have been treated any better. Apart from the food, we drank umpteen glasses of Snowflake beer,

Shenyang wine and *Mao Tai*, a high class brand of spirit, more commonly encountered in its crudest generic form, otherwise known as *Bai Jiu* - a white spirit made from sorghum or maize that was strong enough to strip the lining off your stomach wall and which smelled decidedly wicked. We raised our glasses in toast to every kind of friendship and fellowship you could imagine.Needless to say I got extremely drunk which I think was the main idea before I was dragged back to my room with my legs trailing behind me to sleep it off.

Mission accomplished. I became accustomed to these Chinese banquets and in future just tried to stick to beer which I could manage to control. The Chinese can drink spirits in huge quantities but they cannot seem to consume beer to any large degree. As a former yard of ale champion, I was more than able to hold my own in the drinking stakes provided it was on my terms. After getting up at seven the next day to practise my tai chi and eating breakfast by myself in a banqueting room, I went back to bed for most of the day to sleep it off. Breakfast consisted of two fried eggs, fried noodles, spicy noodles, beef slices with green peppers, cucumbers, salami, steamed buns, dumplings and a large glass of warm sweetened milk - just the fare for a man with a delicate stomach!

After the attention of the first day, they seemed to leave me alone to my own devices on the second day. In the evening I took a stroll around the grounds of the hotel and found that they had a disco up on the top floor. Accessible only by an outside ladder, I scaled the heights and found myself thrown back into the late 1970's. Disco was alive and well! In this small town the locals had hardly ever clapped eyes on a foreigner before, let alone a dancing foreigner. In China, especially amongst young people, the men tended to dance with the men and the girls with the girls - a fact which I was only to discover later. And so it was that the first person who plucked up courage to ask me to dance was a Mongolian peasant. He really fancied himself on the dancefloor but I proceeded to blow him away with my impression of John Travolta in "Saturday Night Fever". They had never seen anything like it before and I found myself being pestered to teach them how to disco dance. By this time, my partner had become quite attached to me and was fiercely protective of his newly acquired amour. I concluded with an amazing dance routine built around some wushu movements when the strobe lights came on and the crowd just melted back in awe. My Mongolian was thrown into paroxysms of delight. I thought he was going to ask me to marry him! I realised it was high time to cool his ardour, so when the music stopped I intimated that I needed to powder my nose and then headed for a drink at the bar. There I managed to get talking to a rather nice young lady called Xi Hua and her friend. Unfortunately my former chaperone spied us and like a jilted lover tried to muscle in on our conversation. I immediately asked Xi Hua to dance, leaving my Mongolian hotpot steaming and fuming on the sidelines. Xi Hua proved to be a much more stimulating conversationalist and smelled a lot better than my sweaty Mongolian partner who hugged me too closely to his armpits for my liking. At 9.20 the late night disco in Fuxin came to an end and we tumbled down the staircase into the street. I stuck closely to my young ladyfriend. The rowdy revellers were intoxicated on a mixture of Coca Cola and disco music. I thought it was all a great blast. I'd been picked up by a man at a disco who had flown into a jealous rage when I had snubbed him for a woman. I only hoped he would not call the Chinese love police and have me arrested for breach of promise. You know what these foreigners are like. Anyway, I bade a fond farewell to Xi Hua and crept back to my room. I intended to get up early for some tai chi practice the next morning so I went to bed almost immediately. No sooner had my head touched the pillow, than my phone rang. No one answered. I put the phone down. In the next hour my phone continued to ring. Sometimes I could hear giggles in the background. Sometimes there was a stony silence. Eventually everything went quiet and I fell asleep with an interesting assortment dreams.

I got up the following morning at 5.30 and headed for Central Park - Fuxin Central Park that is. For a while I strolled around observing the different kinds of tai chi and *Qigong* that people were practising. I found a space and proceeded to practise my form. As usual, a crowd of people gathered to watch. As usual, one of them was a lady English teacher who introduced me to the main tai chi coach in the park whom she addressed as "*Wang Laoshi*" (Teacher Wang). The forms that he knew were the standard 24 and 48 step routines. At this stage I was still impressed by anyone with a Chinese face who taught tai chi. He was a nice enough chap but I soon realised that this teacher in a small provincial town was of limited ability. I had still to meet a teacher of any status in the tai chi world. This did not really worry me as I now had a realistic view of my own ability and felt that there was plenty I could learn from anyone who would agree to teach me. I had still not been formally introduced to the tai chi teacher who had been assigned to me by the local authorities in Fuxin. In view of the fact they had treated me royally from the very first moment that I had set foot in their town, I had no doubt that he would be the best available.

After several more days of rest and relaxation as the guest of the Mayor of Fuxin at the Xi Shan Hotel, I was whisked off to the railway station one afternoon and put on the train to the provincial capital of Liaoning Province, Shenyang, which lay some 200 miles away to the north east. Shenyang is not a city on the normal tourist route although it is the fourth largest city in China after Shanghai, Beijing and Tianjin. It is the industrial hub of the north-eastern provinces, whose prosperity is based on coal, steel and heavy engineering. It has around five million inhabitants and is known affectionately or otherwise by those who live there or those who would never dream of going anywhere near it as "The Armpit of China". I love the place and now regard it as my second or even first home. Anyway, I was now the guest of the Liaoning People's Association for Friendship with Foreign Countries. I was met at Shenyang railway station by a smart young man called Liu Li Wei who spoke immaculate English with a British accent. I was whisked away in a private limousine with my own personal driver, Mr Wang, to the *You Yi Fan Dian*, The Friendship Hotel in the north of the city, handily placed near the vast Beiling Park. I should add at this stage that I had not paid a single penny for my luxury accommodation and transport. It was becoming a little embarrassing. I could not really appreciate what kind of return my Chinese hosts were expecting for their investment. I came to realise that impressing the foreigner with how rich China was, was simply a means of saving face. As a foreign guest, I had to go home able to say that I could not have been treated better anywhere else in the world. At first I revelled in this cosseting but ended up squirming with embarrassment at yet another banquet held in my honour. The crunch finally came when, due to the critical situation in Tian An Men Square, all foreigners were advised by their embassies to leave China. On the eve of our departure, the local authorities in Fuxin insisted on throwing a farewell banquet for us. This was the final straw on the 8th of June. However, I was still back in the heady early days of April 1989.

The following morning Mr Liu and his driver picked me up and took me on some sightseeing of the Northern Imperial Palace. We returned for lunch to the Friendship Hotel when I noted with a high degree of satisfaction that my black limousine, a Toyota Crown, was considerably bigger and smarter than that of the American Consul in Shenyang who happened to be having lunch there that day too. The hotel staff were equally impressed and I was treated with the deference accorded to a visiting head of state. I had to keep reminding myself that I was just a visiting tai chi teacher from England. The purpose of this working lunch was to bring me into contact with two tai chi "masters" as Liu Li Wei described them. In fact when I studied the cards they gave me, I found that they were both coaches. The senior of the two was Luan Xiao Yan, from the Liaoning Physical Education Institute who was also a Liaoning Province Wushu team coach and International Chinese judge. My long term plan was to stay in my twin town of Fuxin for three months and then graduate to the big city life of Shenyang where I would come under the wing of these two teachers sponsored by my hosts : the Liaoning People's Association for Friendship with Foreign Countries. Liu Li Wei confided in me that these were famous masters and that one of them was a former Chinese national tai chi champion. Eventually I lost track of the number of times that I was introduced to "famous masters" and "tai chi champions" during my stay in China with the result that I took such references with a pinch of salt. Although I add hastily that on this occasion it turned out to be true. We proceeded to have an amicable discussion over lunch and arranged to meet the following day for a round of demonstrations.

That afternoon at my request, Liu Li Wei had arranged for me to visit a traditional Chinese medicine hospital. I was introduced to Doctor Liu who showed me the considerable range of his medical skills. We toured the wards together where for the first time I witnessed Qigong being used to treat patients. Doctor Liu transmitted his healing powers through the palm of his hand into the patients' bodies without actually touching them; his hand scanning about an inch or two above the level of the skin. He asked me to place my hand on one patient's skin at the point of treatment. With his hand circling over mine I had a strong warm and tingling sensation, which confirmed in my mind that what I had only read about in Professor Yang En Tang's book about Chinese Qigong Therapy was true. Doctor Liu next took me to see a patient of his who was suffering from bronchitis. This was a frail old lady who turned and smiled wanly at me. Suddenly I felt that although my presence was educational, it was also highly intrusive. I asked Liu Li Wei if the lady did not mind. She shook her head and indicated to me to take a seat and watch. Doctor Liu found the acupuncture points in the lady's back with a swift precision that only comes with a lifetime's practice. He sterilised the skin area and inserted the needles with a deft twist. There was no bleeding and the patient apparently felt no discomfort or pain. Meanwhile he explained to me that whilst treatment in the hospital was principally carried out by traditional methods, it was also supplemented by western drugs. I was pleased to see that whilst in Europe and America, there was an ever growing acceptance of traditional Chinese medicine practice and herbal remedies, western methods were also being employed in China. Not only that, but the hospital authorities were only too pleased to allow a curious foreigner into the intimacies of the treatment rooms without any restrictions. Having practised tai chi for nearly ten years, this was also the first time that I had experienced the sensation of Qi being expressed externally. Whenever I practised tai chi, I certainly felt something internally, an opening of channels, a comfortable warmth, a tingling and numbing sensation. But here was tangible proof that *Qi* could be transmitted from one person to another. Previously I had wanted to believe in its existence. Now I really did believe.

The following day Liu Li Wei returned with the two tai chi coaches/masters. In the grounds of the adjacent provincial government offices, I firstly ran through a performance of my form which took around twenty minutes. I have to say that I felt terribly nervous. My discomfort was added to by the other coach, Mr Yao who continually sucked his teeth and clicked his tongue during my display. Every time he sucked or clicked, I felt that he was indicating a weakness or fault in my form. In hindsight, I realised that my form, which I had carefully practised for all those years, was in fact riddled with faults, but at the time I felt quite pleased and proud of myself. They applauded politely before Luan Xiao Yan gave me his performance of Chen style - the new competition form and the first traditional old long form. I had never seen anything like it in my life. It completely blew my mind. Of course I had read about Chen style but at that time I had never seen anyone performing it, and certainly not anyone of such a high calibre. I knew they wanted to impress me. Well, impress me they did. I thought to myself : This is what I want to learn, this is what I came to China for. I pictured in my mind several years down the road, having learned Chen style tai chi and returning to England where I would equally blow everyone's minds. The thought of this was alluring and completely overpowering. But then reality set in. Could I really aspire to such standards? Was I really at the right stage of development to learn from such advanced teachers? I had my doubts.

Over lunch we discussed my options. I told them that I was honour bound to return to Fuxin for at least a period of several months as I was a guest of the twin town authorities. I added that they would be assigning to me a tai chi teacher who would teach me the 24 step and 48 step routines as well as the 32 step sword form. After this initial period of training I should love to return to Shenyang to study with them. It was at this point that my opinion of the two masters/coaches changed. At the mention of the small provincial town of Fuxin they laughed scornfully and told me there were no good teachers of tai chi in such a backwater. I suddenly had a feeling of resentment rising against them and felt the need to defend the honour of the small town which had made me feel such a special and welcome guest. I owed it to them to defend their good name and honour. Besides, I did not think that belittling other teachers was a particularly generous attitude to take, even if it was true. Maybe in Beijing or Shanghai they could tell me that there were not any good tai chi teachers in a provincial city such as Shenyang. How would Messrs Luan and Yao feel about that? I felt uncomfortable with their demeanour and wondered if these were people I could respect and get along with. Their arrogance lowered them in my estimation. What qualities was I looking for in a tai chi teacher? Obviously a high level of skill and ability but also integrity, humility, dedication, respect and sincerity. The former qualities were obviously there in abundance, but what about the latter? I had my misgivings. The temptation to simply swallow my pride and take the rich easy option open to me was great. They offered to let me study at the Shenyang Sports Institute for three months and then to attend the Chinese National Wushu Championship in Changsha in June. I chose the hard road. It turned out to be the right road in the end. I said a huge thank you to Liu Li Wei and the staff of the Liaoning People's Association. I said goodbye to coaches Liu and Yao, agreeing to meet them again in three months, by which time I felt that I would be better prepared mentally, physically, culturally and linguistically to face up to them. At that moment I was daunted by their superior skills and superior attitude. Maybe the fault lay in my lack of confidence. Maybe it was not them. Maybe it was me. My tai chi sandcastle had been well and truly washed away by the Chinese tide. I needed to rebuild. But from the bottom up. Timing and destiny played a great part in my stay in

China. All along I followed my instincts. They rarely if ever let me down. The experience of living in China proved to be a constant reexamination of self, a constant round of challenges designed to put me to the test. The elements of Yin and Yang were literally in play - to bend with the wind, to turn around and resist, to go with the flow. I had already run the complete spectrum of extremes and emotions in my short stay in China.

I was wracked with doubts about my decision as I waited for the return train to Fuxin in the VIP lounge at Shenyang railway station on the Sunday evening. That afternoon I had watched Italian football on the television in my hotel bedroom, Juventus against Empoli. Juventus won four nil with the former Liverpool striker, Ian Rush, playing at number nine. But the most important news of the day on the early evening news was the death of the former Chinese Communist Party Secretary, Hu Yao Bang at the age of 74. At the time, it did not mean a great deal to me. However, as I was to later experience at first hand the prelude to and the full force of the Tian An Men Square demonstrations and eventual massacre, this item of news loomed in increasing importance. I was so wrapped up in my own thoughts as I waited for the 7.30 train. I did not know if I had made the right decision to return to Fuxin. Or rather in my heart of hearts, I knew it was the right decision. I just had difficulty reconciling myself to that decision. In Shenyang I had been chauffeured around in a car with a driver and an escort. I had stayed at the top hotel, been taken to lunch and dinner, been shown the tourist sights and generally been treated like a VIP. And I had not spent a single penny. In fact, Liu Li Wei even gave me my train ticket from Shenyang back to Fuxin. I was giving all this up. Was I crazy? Perhaps I was.

I was certainly brought back to earth on my first day back in Fuxin. No longer the comforts even of the Xi Shan Hotel. I was now a resident of the Fuxin Mining Institute. I lived in a small room with an alcove containing extremely basic washing facilities which resembled a horse trough, and an open squatting-type toilet in which you put your feet on position in the plates and aimed into the murky depths from a considerable height, paying particular attention to avoid the splashback. On my first Monday morning, I discovered that for some reason the toilet was overflowing all over my floor. By some quirk of logic, however, I was informed that there would be no water flowing through the taps that day. As a rule there was no hot water on Mondays but today there was no water at all. The only time that there was hot water was between 7 and 8 in the evening but you had to get in quickly as the supply was finite and ran out rather quickly. Having subsequently visited the college boiler room, I discovered why. I carry an abiding memory of 7 o'clocks in Fuxin standing by my hot water tap, turned fully on and waiting and listening expectantly for the distant gurgling and trembling of the pipes as the water rushed out in a trickle. Oh, happy days! As a kid, I used to hate to wash. Now at last, at the age of forty my dream had come true.

It came as somewhat of a surprise to find that I was not the only foreigner at the Fuxin Mining Institute. My hometown in England was a mining community so the authorities in their wisdom decided that I would feel most at home there. Besides , the tai chi teacher they had chosen for me was the head of physical education at the Mining Institute, although I had yet to meet him. The other foreigners were some Americans and Canadians who were apparently studying Chinese but whose real motive was to subversively spread the Christian religion among the young students. Of course,this was regarded as a crime by the Chinese authorities and the foreign Bible-bashers would have been summarily thrown out of the country if their ulterior motive had been discovered. My closest friends turned out to be two Germans, Olaf and Andreas from Munich who were mining students completing their thesis on Chinese mining. We shared a love of beer, football and just being crazy together. At lunchtimes I would go to their place and we would drink delicious German coffee they had brought with them and listen to tapes of their favourite German rock band called Bap. If people asked me what I missed most about China, I used to say German coffee and Bap.

Finally it was time for me to meet my tai chi teacher. Because I hardly spoke any Chinese, I had to have an interpreter too. Teacher Qi who had been assigned to give me Chinese lessons sat in on my first few sessions. I was introduced to my teacher as *Tuo Ma Si Xiansheng* - Mister Thomas and he was introduced to me as *Pang Jiaoshou* - Professor Pang. Strangely enough I never found out his full name as I only ever addressed him by his formal title, either *Pang Laoshi* - Teacher Pang or *Pang Jiaoshou*. Professor Pang was quite a short man of about fifty with a shock of black, curly hair which was somewhat unusual. The only other curly-haired Chinese man I knew was Yang En Tang. He had told me that he had been taunted and persecuted during the Cultural Revolution because of his curly locks. As a man of a similar age and generation, I surmised that Professor Pang had undergone a similar humiliation. The most noticeable feature about him was his eyes which seemed to flash and dance as he talked animatedly. He smiled a lot too when he talked although he rarely seemed to laugh. He gave me the impression of a very amiable shark. Through my interpreter, Pang told me that he would first teach me the basic 24 step tai chi routine and proceeded to give me a performance. For a man of his age, he was extremely supple and fluent in his movements. His stances were very low and his kicks impressively and effortlessly high. Like many wushu athletes, he came from a background in gymnastics when he was young. What most impressed me about him was his spirit. His face and his whole body exuded an expression of tremendous energy being translated into the form. Not only that, but the form bore the stamp of his own personality. He was so aware and yet so focused. As he brought his feet together at the end of the form, I could not help smiling broadly. I am a person who naturally smiles a lot. He turned to me and smiled too. He gave me a crunching handshake and that was it. We were the best of friends. I told teacher Qi that I would try to manage without his help as an interpreter. While in Beijing I had bought two books at the Foreign Language Bookstore in *Wangfujing* - one on simplified tai chi and the other on the 48 step routine and 32 tai chi sword. This was my syllabus for the next three months. I felt that it would help to bond our relationship if we worked together by ourselves rather than tolerate the intrusiveness of a third party. If I had any serious questions, I could ask teacher Qi later for his assistance. Meanwhile I could use the books I had bought plus any notes I had made to help me revise and practise.

And practice I did. Professor Pang really ripped into the form. In our first lesson he taught me the first eight movements - a third of the form. To be honest this was too much for me. I am a slow learner at the best of times and prefer to take things very steadily. I think he was simply overeager to please. After each movement he would correct my posture and say, "*Hao, hao*" (Good, good). We continued to smile a lot but the lack of easy conversation became a growing frustration to me. Without the power of language to communicate with your teacher, how could you learn to any great extent? Of course, I could copy his movements and eventually would be able to practise the whole form. But this was simply the bare bones and what I needed was some meat.

The day after my first lesson, I woke up with a terrible sore throat. This may have been due to the fact that the previous evening there had been no hot water at seven o'clock and I took a shower in freezing cold water. Or it could have been as a result of the ailment which frequently hits foreigners in Liaoning province - a severe hacking cough caused by the dry, windy atmosphere and appalling air pollution. This area was reputed to be the second most polluted on earth.Why, I asked myself couldn't we be number one? If you are going to live in an extremely unhealthy environment, you might as well have the satisfaction of being the world champions! Anyway, as a result of my illness I went along to the college clinic and my lesson was suspended for that day. I was given an assortment of traditional Chinese medicine to take, including three pills I had to take three times a day, one pill I had to take four times a day and ten pills I had to take twice a day. Having to think so carefully about when next to take my medicine took my mind completely off my razor blade throat and hacking cough.

Miraculously the next day the cough had vanished and I was able to get back to my tai chi lessons. This time we only learned six new moves and the day after that only four. The day after, we were back to six and before I knew it, we had finished the whole form in less than a week. The following week Professor Pang left me completely alone to practise by myself. I took advantage of this respite to step up my Chinese lessons with teacher Qi. The next time I met Professor Pang I wanted to be able to speak some Chinese and to actually asked him some incisive questions. Every evening I poured over my Chinese homework and practised writing my Chinese characters. The next time we met I said to him,"*Hao jiu bu jian le*" (Long time no see) at which he burst into convulsions of laughter. I followed that up with "*Ni hao ma*?" (How are you?) and concluded with "*Ni baba, mama dou hao ma*?" (How are your Mum and Dad?) which really sent him into such fits of laughter that I thought he was going to choke. I carried on regardless, determined to have my say "*Mang bu mang*?" (Are you busy?) "*Lei bu lei*?" (Are you tired?) "*Leng bu leng*?" (Are you cold?) were some of the pearls of questions that I threw at him. I ended up by saying "*Dong bu dong*?" (Do you understand?) and finally "*Xie xie, zai jian.*" (Thank you, goodbye.) He just could not take it any more and ran off spluttering in the direction of the boiler room. I did not know which was going to explode first, the boiler or him. Hm, lesson over for today, I thought.

That evening I burnt the midnight oil with my Chinese and tai chi notes. I asked teacher Qi to write down all the names of the movements in the 24 step form in Chinese and recorded their pronunciation onto my recording walkman. I spent the entire evening in my room practising each of the movements individually and memorising their Chinese names. The time for the next day's lesson arrived and I was ready. I made sure I was there first and stood with my feet together and my arms hanging loose and relaxed by my side in the ready position. As Professor Pang appeared, I announced "*Kai bu, qi shi*" (Opening step, commencing form). I proceeded to perform the routine with a running commentary in Chinese. Professor Pang just stood there with his arms folded across his chest. I concluded with "*Shizi shou, shou shi*" (Cross hands, closing form). I brought my left foot up slowly beside my right, inclined at the waist in a bow and gave a martial arts salute. Professor Pang nodded his head and said "*Haojile*" (Excellent). "*Danshi you jige wenti*" (But there are some problems). This was just what I wanted to hear, not only praise but constructive criticism. We spent the rest of the lesson and in fact the rest of the week ironing out my problems.

I spoke more and more Chinese daily. As I did so, Professor Pang took me more and more seriously. If there was something I did not understand, I made him write it down and I checked it out with teacher Qi later. I practised fiercely. Everyone was impressed. Some Chinese students even asked me if I would teach them tai chi. This was a great accolade and as a result I practised even more fiercely. They said that I liked to "*Chi Ku*" (吃苦) which literally means to eat bitterness. I was willing to endure hardship and work hard in order to achieve my goals. I knew this was only the simplified 24 steps tai chi form but I wanted to demonstrate my dedication and application to my teacher. Besides, I knew that practice and correct practice was one of the keys to improvement and access to a higher level. I realised that I was a relative novice but that a strong foundation in the fundamentals of tai chi principles had to be laid in order to build a stronger tai chi castle than the one I had built in England. Professor Pang became less praising and more critical. He pulled me up on every small point and would insist that I practise over and over again until I had performed it to his complete satisfaction. I preferred this stern, severe approach to the former amiable, easygoing approach. After a week's practice in this vein my tai chi skeleton had some real meat on it.

That weekend Professor Pang spoke the words that I had been waiting to hear, "*Lian Jian*" (Let's practise sword). With the 24 step form now safely tucked under my belt, my teacher felt that it was time for me to get to grips with tai chi sword. I had heard from the other students at the Institute that Professor Pang was regarded as an excellent swordsman and that this was his real forte. I could not contain my excitement and could not wait to get the weapon in my hand. On Saturday afternoon, I turned up early at the appointed place. Not long after, Professor Pang appeared carrying his sword, a battered old blade with a rusty hilt and faded tassel. The handguard was loose and rattled like an old bicycle chain. He seemed to sense my disappointment and with a sudden rapid twirling action, the lifeless sword was spinning and flashing in the sunlight so fast that it eventually became a red and silver blur with the tassel flying closely behind like the tail of a comet. Professor Pang's eyes flashed and glinted with equal ardour. He finally came to an abrupt halt with a flourish and struck a pose with the sword thrust skywards where it continued to tremble and vibrate with resonating energy for some considerable time. I watched in awe, completely captivated by this display. As I stood rooted to the spot, Professor Pang went to a nearby tree, snapped off a low straight branch, stripped it of twigs, returned and thrust it into my hand. "*Nide jian*" (This is your sword) he said. And so I began to learn the standard 32 step tai chi sword form with my branch. It did not seem to matter that I did not have a real sword, as it just served to underline my novice status. If I had a real sword, people would expect me to handle it as expertly as Professor Pang. By the following weekend, however, when we were about half way through the form, I cycled into town and came across a sports shop. There on the second floor I found a bundle of swords tied up in the corner. The quality was not terribly high but the sword I picked out was well-balanced and felt comfortable in my hand. I asked the assistant "*Duo shao qian*?" (How much is it?) She replied "*Er shi er kuai wu.*" (22 yuan 50) which was a ridiculously low price of around two English pounds. I had the assistant wrap my sword up in paper and string then cycled back to the Institute with my precious package. Back in my room, I ripped open the packing, gripped my sword, gave it a twirl and promptly knocked my mug of tea onto the floor and took a chunk of wood out of my desk. From that moment on, I learnt to show my sword rather more respect.

It is important at this point to sketch in some of the background of what was happening in China at this time. I had reached the midpoint of learning tai chi sword. It was the last weekend of April, Saturday the 29th and Sunday the 30th. Monday the 1st of May was May Day and a National Holiday to commemorate International Labour Day. Thursday the 4th of May marked the 70th anniversary of the founding of the May Fourth Movement. At the conclusion of the First World War, the allies had transferred Germany's rights of occupation in Shandong Province to Japan. This decision sparked off a massive 300,000 strong student-led demonstration in Beijing, aimed at the humiliating treatment meted out to China by the western allies and at the weak and submissive Beijing government for accepting this decision. It was one of the first expressions of Chinese nationalism. During this period, the nation-wide movement of students, workers and intellectuals demanded that China should be treated by other nations as an independent, sovereign state and that domestic reforms involving the abolition of feudal practices and the democratisation of laws should be introduced. This was thus a highly charged period of significance in the modern history of China, particularly in the hearts of young Chinese people. In a historical parallel, a group of students had begun to protest in Tian An Men Square, Beijing. Among other things, they were demanding an end to corruption and greater freedom of expression. They wanted to make their views heard. Around the 20th of April there had been 25,000 students on the Square. Now by the 1st of May, there were 150,000. Students were pouring in from all over the country. Fuxin was only a small provincial town with no universities. The Coalmining Institute was the principal seat of learning. The students of the Institute were none the less fervent and were determined to show their solidarity with their fellow students. Fortunately, Fuxin only lay some five hours by train from the capital and so was easily accessible. The Institute's hierarchy looked down on any political involvement of their students. This did not dissuade regular student delegations from travelling to Beijing to participate actively on the Square and to bring back the latest news which they posted on the walls on large notices called *Da Zi Bao* all over the campus. As I went about my daily tai chi practice, I saw groups of students huddled around the posters in animated discussion. At night the Institute authorities would rip down the posters but they would be replaced by new ones in the morning. The normal relaxed air of the campus was gradually giving way to an underlying tension and expectant excitement. We foreigners continued to go about our business, learning Chinese, studying Chinese mining methods and practising tai chi. But the atmosphere began to take on an air of unreality. My diaries concerning this remarkable period will be related in greater detail in a later book in this series. Suffice it to say, something was about to happen and something big.

I continued to learn tai chi sword with Professor Pang and by Friday 12th of May had finished the routine. I carried on practising by day but in the evenings we were glued to our TV sets watching the Chinese CCTV early evening news and listening to the BBC World Service and the Voice of America on our short-wave radios. Tai Chi was still important to me but was being increasingly pushed into the background as events on Tian An Men Square unfurled. On Saturday the 13th of May the hunger strike began.This coincided with Gorbachev's state visit to meet Deng Xiao Ping. There were 500,000 people on the Square. Everyone started to get a little crazy. Thursday the 18th of May was supposed to be the Institute's Sports Day. No one turned up. The entire student body boycotted the event and declared an all-out strike in sympathy with their fellow students in Beijing. Olaf, Andreas and I drank beer all day and all night. There were now a million people on the Square. For reasons I can no longer remember I cut chunks of my hair off and stopped shaving. I bought a huge potted plant and put it in my window. It completely blocked out the light. Andreas went into the bathroom and cut half of his moustache off, too. Nobody felt like eating. Prime Minister Li Peng met student leaders including Wu Er Kai Xi in the Great Hall of the People. It was all on television. It was like an epic film and we all had walk-on parts. There were a million people on Tian An Men Square. It seemed as if there were a million people on the streets of Fuxin that afternoon as the two German students and I went into the square in the centre of town which was dominated by a huge statue of Mao Ze Dong with his arm raised in inspiration and exhortation. We climbed to the very tops of lampposts, clapping, cheering and giving V signs to the ranks of students and workers as they paraded by. We saluted them and they applauded us back. As we returned to the Institute we were closely followed by the police.

The following day, Friday the 19 of May, all the foreigners were called into the Institute's Foreign Affairs Office where Director Yao gave us a severe warning as to our future behaviour. The striking students, especially the 300 who had travelled to Beijing the night before, would be reprimanded and disciplined. The current problems were internal to China and were none of our business. We should not get involved in any way. Our stay in China was short. They would have to live there when all of this was over. He advised us to stay away from all the places where people gathered. It was not safe for us. We should not take photographs. We should stay in our living rooms and classrooms and continue our studies as normal. We should not mix with the students and should definitely not visit their dormitories. We should not go out at all after dark. Our safety could not be assured. If we did not already appreciate it, the gravity of the situation was certainly spelled out to us now. On Saturday the 20th of May, martial law was declared in parts of Beijing. That evening on the BBC World Service, British citizens were advised not to visit China. Those already in China were told not to visit the large cities. Meanwhile, in England there was a heatwave, although in my home county of Yorkshire there were heavy freak floods. In some homes the water was eight feet deep. The rest of the country was enjoying its warmest May for 25 years. I was on the other side of the earth in a country whose fabric seemed to be disintegrating before my very eyes. I did not know if I was drowning or suffocating.

My classes had been suspended for a week. However, on Monday 22nd of May Professor Pang knocked on my door and told me we were going to start learning the 48 step tai chi form. He did not say a word about the political situation. I honestly did not feel like carrying on. My heart was not in it but I complied with his instructions. I no longer knew why I was learning tai chi. It seemed such a ludicrously insignificant thing to be doing in such momentous times. My classes took on an air of surrealism. I felt like a zombie being drilled through a sequence of inconsequential movements. The names of the movements themselves began to take on bizarre and doom-laden connotations in my deranged mind. All the foreigners were beginning to suffer from mild paranoia. Lean Obliquely, White Snake Puts Out Its Tongue, Pat Foot To Subdue The Tiger. The emotional strain was starting to tell. Turn Left To Strike, Strike Opponent's Ears With Both Fists, Strike With Hidden Fist. A sinister imminence of dark repression and disaster was in the air. There was a block on all international telephone calls so we were not allowed to contact our families. All our incoming mail was opened. We were becoming prisoners. Prisoners in China and prisoners in our own minds. At least we still had each other for moral support, but not for much longer. The hammer blow came for me on Thursday the 25th of May. Olaf and Andreas were due to leave. My mates were leaving. Their course had finished. They were going to take the train to Beijing and then fly back to Germany. I wanted to beg them to stay and see it out with me, but I didn't. Their train left just after midday. We drank beer and listened to the news on the radio all morning. Andreas went into the bathroom and shaved off the other half of his moustache, put the shavings in an envelope and gave them to me. It was an unbearable farewell. Our hugs on the southbound platform of Fuxin railway station could not have been more heartfelt. As the train disappeared into the distance, I just did two movements from the tai chi form : Needle At Sea Bottom and Flash The Arm to send them on their way. I cycled back to the Institute in the dreary afternoon sunshine with heavy legs and an even heavier heart. Once in my room, I picked up my sword, twirled it around uncontrollably, hacking and thrashing anything that got in my way. I did not care any more. When my wrist gave out and I could not twirl any more, I threw myself sobbing on my bed.

On Friday the 26th of May, I met Professor Pang once more for my lesson. I decided the only way to stay sane and to deal with this situation on a personal level was to channel everything I was feeling into my tai chi. Here was an ideal vehicle to restore some balance, tranquillity and peace of mind. By a quirk of fate this coincided with our study of Waving Hands Like Clouds and Parting The Horse's Mane which seemed highly appropriate to my mood. I did not say a word throughout the entire lesson. Neither did Professor Pang. Each of us knew what the other was thinking. Whereas at first, the inadequacy of my spoken Chinese had been a barrier to our communication, now the sheer intensity of our silence spoke more eloquently than any words could have done in Chinese or any other spoken language. We practised the form together in perfect harmony. Never before and never since have I felt such an emotional high and an intensity of energy running through my body. It was magical. At the end of the session we parted and I returned to my room. I sat down at my desk facing the window which was still shrouded by the huge pot plant. The energy was still crackling through my body. I closed my eyes and held my sword tightly in front of me in both hands. I don't know how long I stayed like this. What I do know is that then something remarkable and extraordinary happened. I heard a noise but did not dare to open my eyes. A few moments later I heard the same noise again. This time I could not resist it. I had squeezed my eyes so tightly shut that at first my vision was blurred. I rubbed my eyes and opened them fully. There on the desk in front of me, the two largest leaves from my plant had turned yellow and dropped dead. I heaved an enormous sigh. I had to face it. My two best friends had gone.

The weather was changing dramatically. On Sunday the 28th it was 33 degrees and by Wednesday the 31st it was 35 degrees. That is 95 degrees Fahrenheit. The cauldron was beginning to boil towards a crescendo. On Thursday the 1st of June, there was a blackout on foreign reporters sending their stories out of the country. On Friday the 2nd, the Autonomous Federation of Beijing Workers set up a tent on Tian An Men Square and broadcast illegal messages disclaiming the actions of the Beijing Daily and denounced it as a hard-line organ of the government and labelling it "Li Peng's poodle". Four celebrities joined the hunger strike, including three intellectuals and a famous pop singer Hou De Jian from Taiwan. On Saturday the 3rd, I learned four more moves of the 48 step form as far as Apparent Close-Up. Tear gas was used for the first time on the Square and there were running fights with the military outside the Great Hall of the People. Not only was the weather hot but it was dry and windy too. As I returned to my room after my lesson, a whole window was blown out of an office on the third floor. It crashed to the ground, smashing to smithereens just missing me. The country was in upheaval. The elements were in turmoil. During all this period of intoxicated freedom, one song had emerged capturing the mood of the time:*Gen Zhe Gan Jue Zou* (Follow Your Feelings) sung by Zhang Hang. It was on all the students' lips. They would hum the tune and sing the words wherever they went. It was blasted out of the tannoy systems and loudspeakers on campuses, in offices and in factories. The first line of the song went "*Jin zhua zhu meng de shou*" (Grasp the hand of the dream). We were all grasping the hand tightly but the dream was fading and slipping inevitably from our grasp. Even my tai chi was slipping through my fingers, turning into an uncontrollable beast which taunted me with a forecast of impending doom. On the eve of June the 4th I learned form 31 *Shang Bu Qin Da* (Step Forward To Strike). This was followed by form 32 *Ru Feng Si Bi* (Apparent Close-Up). The fate was sealed. I knew it was all over. At 2 a.m. the tanks rolled into Tian An Men Square and the massacre took place.

Monday the 5th of June was a dreary day. Students at the Institute stood with their faces uplifted in the pouring rain singing patriotic songs. They massed at 8 a.m. to form a march headed by wreaths for those who had died in Beijing, including it was rumoured four students from Fuxin. Unlike before, this time I did not want to join their demonstration. This was their moment of grief, their moment of history. It would be inappropriate of me to intrude. Where were the heady days of elation only two weeks before when 3,000 students had marched through the streets of Fuxin and besieged the government offices. I had been there. This was now the bloody reality of revolution. Oh, yes, and by the way, I heard on the news Ayatollah Khomeini died today. The students have gone on indefinite strike. Many of them have gone home. They have heard that in places like Shenyang, troops have surrounded the university campuses to prevent students from leaving. The Institute has an empty feel. Fuxin is turning into a ghost town. Whereas before everyone was on the streets, now they have retreated indoors, closed their shutters and bolted their doors to the outside world. The revolution is dead, it would seem, at least in Fuxin.

Director Yao called all the remaining foreigners into his office to lay down a strict code of conduct we had to follow. At lunchtime all the talk was of leaving. I felt that my Chinese adventure was over. The only questions remaining were how to leave and when to leave. By train to Shenyang then fly to Guangzhou and so on to Hong Kong. By bus to Dalian then catch a boat to Shanghai. We daren't risk going directly to Beijing. On the BBC no specific instructions were given to British citizens inside China. However, on the Voice of America, I heard the US Ambassador advising all Americans to leave China as the country was on the verge of civil war as the military factions divided up and took sides. On Wednesday the 7th of June it was Derby Day in Britain - the biggest horse race in the calendar. I listened on the BBC World Service. Security would be tight around Epsom Racecourse for the visit of the Queen and the royal family. All police leave had been cancelled to ensure control of the large crowds. I couldn't stop myself from laughing. I just found everything so ludicrous. The British Foreign Secretary said on the news, "I urge the Chinese government to come to its senses." Even more preposterous! The Chinese government thought that it had come to its senses. On the television the CCTV 7 o'clock news was now showing pictures in black and white from Beijing but only of student misdeeds - throwing petrol bombs, burning trucks and buses, beating up soldiers, overturning armoured vehicles, stoning their occupants to death then incinerating their bodies. The pictures were graphic and gruesome. I couldn't sleep at all that night.

I got up at 5 on Thursday the 8th of June. At first it was only grey and overcast. Then it started to rain. The BBC was telling all British citizens to get out. Now! And still it rained. It had never rained so long and hard since I had been in China. I took my sword and went to my usual practice ground. Soaked to the skin and trembling with cold and fear, I practised without ceasing until I could practise no more. What was it all for? I didn't know. But I had to cling onto something. That lunchtime all the foreigners gathered to eat together. We gorged ourselves on all the luxuries we had been saving for a rainy day - cheese, jam, sausages, the lot. Well hell it was raining now! So let's eat. We ate and drank everything we had until we were all heartily sick.

In the afternoon, I received a visit from my friend , Zhao Juan from the Fuxin City Foreign Affairs Office. As I was a guest of the town, the Mayor wanted to invite me to a farewell banquet. I could not believe it. It was just too ludicrous for words. In the circumstances it was inappropriate to say the least. Zhao Juan begged me, saying they would be insulted if I refused. The country was on the verge of civil war and they wanted to throw a banquet in my honour. It was a question of saving face and keeping up appearances to the bitter end, as if nothing had happened. Chinese traditions die very hard indeed. A car picked me up and whisked me off to my old dancing ground of the Xi Shan Hotel. In the private banqueting room, I counted twenty-one dishes then stopped counting. We drank beer and Maotai in abundance. I started to loosen up and got drunk. For the first time in many days, in many weeks, I actually felt like myself. They presented me with some cushion covers. They were yellow - the colour reserved for the Emperor. They had dragons embroidered on the corners. We raised our glasses and toasted everlasting friendship. I felt glad now that I had gone after all. I really loved these people. I wanted to stay but in my heart I knew I had to leave. Back home the CCTV news began with Prime Minister Li Peng. This was his first public appearance since Sunday. It was a symbol that he was now firmly in control. He looked relaxed and delivered a spirited , rousing speech. I knew I had to leave.

Friday the 9th of June dawned. The beer and spirit had done the trick. For the first time in as long as I could remember, I had slept. It was all arranged. We would take the afternoon train to Shenyang. From there we would fly to Guangzhou in the south and cross the border to safety in Hong Kong. That was our plan of escape. We packed hurriedly and waited outside the Institute's Foreign Affairs Office for the cars that would take us to the railway station. It was hard to know what to say. Everyone stood silently, holding each other for comfort. I only had two Chinese phrases in my mind, "*Dui bu qi*" (I'm sorry) and "*Wo dei zoule*" (I have to go). Our friends from outside the Institute had heard the news that we were leaving. They dropped by to say farewell and have their photographs taken with us one last time. It was nigh impossible to smile and pose for the cameras.

I had been wondering where Professor Pang was. I didn't really expect to see him again. At that very moment, he rode up on his bike. He grabbed my hand and said "*Lian tai ji quan ba*" (Let's practise tai chi). I unpacked my sword and we ran through the routine a couple of times and then practised the 48 step form as far as move 32, Apparent Close-Up. We had never finished the routine. He then said something that I could not quite catch. "What did he say?" I asked one of the young English-speaking Chinese students. He said, "Please come back some day and finish learning the form." This was more than I could take. I hugged Professor Pang tightly, the tears welling up in my eyes. Zhao Juan put her arms around me but I felt desolate, inconsolable. I had to go back into the office where my emotions got the better of me and I cried openly. When I went back outside, Professor Pang had gone. All the foreigners piled into the limousines and the convoy slowly set off on its way. The wave of emotion was simply unbearable. The departure of the foreigners was heavy with significance. It was as if the heart had been ripped out of the Institute. To the Chinese students we were a talisman. We represented a better life - something they could believe in and strive for. In their minds we represented freedom, democracy and human rights. But we were leaving. Everyone was crying now. Zhao Juan thrust a card into my hand. It said "Time is short, but friendship between us is everlasting. Your Chinese friend - Zhao Juan."

I'm sorry. I can't write any more. Please forgive me. "*Dui bu qi. Wo dei zoule.*"

GETTING OUT AND GETTING BACK

On Saturday the 10th of June 1989, I left China by train from Guangzhou en route to Hong Kong. The scene at Guangzhou Railway Station was bedlam. It was as if the entire population of China was trying to leave. At the border control we could change our FEC's into Hong Kong dollars but we were stuck with our Chinese currency, the *Renminbi*. We had to spend it or throw it away. So as a last gesture we blew it all at the Guangzhou Friendship Store on fancy Chinese bowls, plates and tea services. Even the china was leaving China!

I had never been to Hong Kong before. We arrived in the early evening. As we emerged through Kowloon into the harbour, the view was mind-blowing. I had been living in the twilight world of China where lightbulbs were 40 watts, there was minimal street lighting and no one used their bicycle, car or bus headlights for fear of using up the battery. I was completely dazzled by the lights of the neon signs and the floodlit waterfront skyscrapers. Hong Kong was one hour behind Beijing time but I felt that I had actually travelled a hundred years forward in time.

We split up and I found lodgings at the appropriately named Promised Land Hostel managed by Miss Gloria Wong in Bute Street just off Nathan Road in Mongkok. Having deposited my things, I tumbled back out into Nathan Road and took the number two bus back down to the harbour terminus. There I boarded the Star Ferry for Hong Kong island - a twenty-five cent ride across the bay and surely the most breathtaking sight in the world. Fuxin by night this was not! I could not help but be excited, although I tried desperately to suppress these feelings of elation. I had escaped but my Chinese friends had not. I felt as if I were walking around with the word "Deserter" tattooed on my forehead. I had never felt so ashamed in my life. I made my way to the 24-hour cable and wireless office. I bought a fifty Hong Kong dollar phone card which would give me four minutes of time to England. I dialled my family's number. "Hi, it's Howard. Do you still remember me? You sound so close. I'll see you in a week. Perhaps. Love you. Bye."

In fact I spent a further ten days in Hong Kong, waiting and hoping. I wasn't really sure what for. I supposed for entry clearance to go back into China. To rejoin my friends. To continue my Chinese adventure. It had only just begun. How could it have so cruelly been cut short? At least I could console myself with the fact that I had been to China, if only for three months. Anyway if I did go back, things could not possibly be the same again. Could they? My plans were in tatters. My life was in tatters. Where could I go from here? I continued to watch and listen as events unfolded further on the mainland. I bought the glossy magazines and T-shirts decrying the brutal atrocities perpetrated by the repressive Chinese regime. I supported the Hong Kong students hunger-striking in sympathy and solidarity with their fellow students in China. But I ate at McDonald's and I drank English beer in the pubs. I attended the mass demonstration in Victoria Park where we all wore black arm bands and cheered as a giant replica of the Goddess of Democracy similar to the one in Tian An Men Square was erected. But I shopped in Tsim Sha Tsui night market and bought a fake Rolex watch. I hoped and I prayed that what had been done could be undone. But I watched the Hong Kong Dragon Boat Racing Festival in Hong Kong harbour, in which the Chinese men's team from Guangzhou defeated allcomers. I cried and I laughed. With the hurt and the pain. And I cried again. But I bought the plane ticket and after ten days I went home. To England. I was reminded of the Chinese idiom : *San Shi Liu Ji, Zou Wei Shang Ji* (三十六计，走为上计) - Among the 36 strategies, leaving is the best. In other words, sometimes the best solution is just to leave.

No sooner had I set foot in England than I feverishly began plotting my return to China. I realised that I could not tread the same path as before, emotionally, morally, financially or realistically. However, I did have contacts and I set about renewing them. My home town had severed links with its Chinese twin of Fuxin expressly against my advice. The local authorities felt that they simply had to follow the hostile wave of political and public opinion against China. The Yorkshire China Services Centre had also broken economic, cultural and educational ties with Liaoning Province. Nevertheless, I launched a wave of correspondence off my own bat at the Liaoning People's Association for Friendship with Foreign Countries and my young British English-speaking friend Liu Li Wei. I reminded him of their invitation for me to travel on to Shenyang to study with Masters Luan and Yao and to attend the Shenyang Institute of Physical Culture. I was greeted with silence. I had no way of knowing if my letters had got through or been intercepted, if they had been received and ignored, or if they had been put in a tray marked "pending". The uncertainty was unbearable. In view of the continued silence, I had to explore other avenues.

In mainland China there are six elite Institutes of Physical Culture - Beijing, Shanghai, Shenyang, Xian, Chengdu and Wuhan. I decided to write to two of them, Beijing and Shanghai. The Beijing Institute replied that they were organising an International Wushu training class for foreign students between July the 20th and August the 10th 1989. There were three levels of study -elementary, intermediate and judge class. As far as the tai chi was concerned, the best they could offer was the 48 form, the 32 sword form and the short 36 Chen style form. The classes would be taught by high level coaches and professors including Zhang Wen Guang, Cheng Chuan Ru and Men Hui Feng. The cost would be fifty US dollars a day inclusive of tuition, food and accommodation. So the three week course would cost around a thousand dollars plus my return flight to Beijing. It did not really meet my requirements. The Shanghai Institute replied that they did not accept foreign undergraduate students. They did have a short-term wushu training programme for foreign friends which would be held from May 1st to June 10th. However, they informed me and I quote, "But most of the students are green hand while you are an expert. What do you think of that ?" I must say that I was flattered at being called an expert after practising tai chi in England for only ten years and in China for barely three months. The letter made me chuckle but I declined the offer. Later in 1989 the Beijing Institute offered to give me a place as a self-sponsored foreign student at various levels ranging from that of a general advanced student at US$2500 a year up to that of a doctorate student at US$5000 a year for tuition alone. As an impoverished English tai chi teacher, I had to decline this offer too.

The year of 1989 rolled on. It looked as if I was out of luck. I began to fall back into my English way of life. Then unexpectedly I received a New Year's card from the Liaoning People's Association for Friendship with Foreign Countries. They acknowledged my earlier correspondence. My English-speaking guide from within the Association, Liu Li Wei, had been transferred. My case was now being dealt with by someone else. They had passed on my letter to the Liaoning Province Sports Commission. For the first time in six months the aura of doom and gloom that had settled over my existence began to lift. I could see a small ray of hope in my future. International relations with China were still cool but the memory of Tian An Men Square was fading, although not in my mind. The USA dithered over renewing its Most Favoured Nation Trading Status with China. Eventually economic reality won the day over moral and emotional misgivings. China was once again being accepted into the international fold. My home town steadfastly refused to renew ties with its Chinese counterpart of Fuxin despite my pleading on their behalf. However, the Yorkshire China Services Centre did start up in business again, so opening the door to economic, educational and cultural exchanges once more. Nearly a year after I had set foot in China for the first time, the opportunity presented itself for the second time. On this occasion, I determined that whatever happened I would not leave under any circumstances.

The first part of my journey was reassuringly familiar. On Wednesday the 2nd of May 1990, I boarded the same Pakistan Airlines flight as the previous year. In the dead of night we flew over Tehran. This time the flight was as smooth as silk. On board there was a twenty-strong group of British birdwatchers who were heading for China, hoping for some unusual sightings of the feathered variety. Their main destination was Beidaihe on the Bohai seacoast to the northeast of Beijing. When they asked me if I had any advice, I simply told them not to accept any offers to dance from sweaty Mongolian peasants. Stick to the birds!

On arrival at Beijing Airport I knew what to do this time. I went straight up to the airport bus desk and said *"Lai yige"* (Give me one) and for seven yuan I received a bus ticket to the centre of Beijing. This feeling of confidence was highly reassuring but I have to admit that I missed the dangerous edge of not knowing what to do that I had experienced on my first trip. I booked into the Sports Hotel near Tian Tan Park precisely as before, only this time I didn't get lost on my evening stroll. In the morning I went to the park in search of Master Yang and his group of tai chi students I had met the previous year. But they were nowhere to be found. I visited Tian An Men Square which superficially bore no signs of the epic struggle that had taken place there on June the 4th of 1989. The enormous portrait of Mao Ze Dong still looked benignly down from the north side of the square just beside the entrance to the Forbidden City. On closer inspection, you could see some bullet holes in the masonry and the faint remains of tank tracks on the paving stones. But to all intents and purposes you would not have known what historic events had taken place there barely a year before, unless you had seen them with your own eyes, witnessed the vivid images unfolding on your television screen or known students who had been here, some of whom had returned and some who had not.

I had felt guilty about leaving China. Now strangely enough I felt guilty about coming back. It was as if my return was a tacit approved of the actions of the Chinese government and a betrayal of my friends in Fuxin. When I looked around Tian An Men Square and saw the young couples posing for photographers with their bright, smiling children dressed in their Young Pioneer uniforms and fathers proudly carrying babies wearing replica army hats, it was hard to remember and even harder to imagine the hatred that people had felt towards the government leadership, Prime Minister Li Peng and elder statesman Deng Xiao Ping and especially the People's Liberation Army which had been turned against its own people. I narrowed my eyes in the sunlight and stood there motionless for a very long time. In the haze I saw the makeshift tents, the scaffolding and platforms made of bamboo from which the student leaders, Wang Dan, Wu Er Kai Xi and Cai Ling made their impassioned speeches. I heard the laughter, the sound of guitars and the patriotic student songs. I saw the flags and banners waving, daubed with slogans of hope and freedom. I saw the giant statue made by the students, the Goddess of Democracy, holding the torch of freedom. I saw the Chinese characters painted boldly in red below - *Minzhu Zhi Shen* (民主之神). And then I heard the sound of gunfire and saw the tanks. I blinked for a moment and it was all gone. Ordinary people walked by, oblivious to my feelings. They seemed happy and carefree. At least on the outside. Chinese people are good at enduring hardship and just getting on with life. Why could't I just let go of the past and get on with my life. I put my things on the floor, took off my coat and proceeded to perform the 24 step tai chi routine. I just felt completely numb. Unusually this time nobody stood and watched.

No crowd gathered. It was just me alone with my feelings. It was only when I reached Snake Creeps Down that I felt my burden of guilt beginning to lift.Golden Cock Stands On One Leg. Work The Shuttles On Both Sides. And then forms 19 and 20: Needle At Sea Bottom followed by Flash The Arm. I remembered that I had used these two movements on Fuxin railway station to say goodbye to my German friends Olaf and Andreas when they had departed for Beijing. Turn Deflect, Parry And Punch. Apparent Close-up. Cross Hands. Closing Form. As I pushed down finally with my hands and breathed out deeply, I felt a sense of release. I no longer felt so alone. The ghosts and echoes of those million people were with me now. I turned and walked away slowly. I did not want to be on the Square to witness the setting of the sun over the Great Hall of the People, as the red flecks on the edge of the sun finally burnt out for another day.

On Friday the 4th of May I visited Beijing Railway Station to buy my train ticket for Shenyang. Nothing had changed in the intervening period. At the International Passengers Booking Office, the clerks were as surly and unhelpful as before and they still didn't speak any English. It didn't matter to me this time as I spoke enough Chinese now to get by. In fact I was able to help out several foreign travellers who were on their first visit and were as just lost as I had been the previous year. I bought a ticket for next morning's train leaving at 6:34 which was due in Shenyang at 5:50 in the evening. The rest of the day I spent shopping in Wangfujing, the main shopping street in Beijing, which now boasted the biggest McDonald's in the world on its corner. I bought some books at the Foreign Language Bookstore, including a book on Yang style by Yang Zhen Duo and one on Chen style by Chen Xiao Wang. Having returned to my hotel I phoned the Foreign Affairs Office of the Liaoning Province Physical Culture Commission and informed my contact, Li Yu Min, of my time of arrival so he could pick me up at the station. On Saturday 5th of May I boarded train number 11 bound for Shenyang. Even by express it was nearly a twelve hour journey. I had plenty of time to contemplate both my past and my future in China. The train to Shenyang did not pass through Fuxin. I viewed this as a mixed blessing. One half of me was dying to return. The other half was filled with dread and foreboding with what I might find, how I might be received and how I might feel. The wounds were beginning to heal. I didn't want them to be reopened. Now was not the right time to go back. Would there ever be a right time? It was usually a mistake to return to a place where one had experienced either emotional highs or lows. I didn't want to forget. But for the moment I needed to forget in order to get on with the rest of my life.

On my first visit to China I had been an all-expenses paid guest. This time I had to work for my living and pay my own way. My sponsors, the Liaoning Province Physical Culture Commission had arranged for me to teach English at the Northeast University, one of the key universities in China, situated in the south of Shenyang near Nan Hu

Park. The problem was that no one had bothered to inform the university authorities. And to put it bluntly, they didn't want me as they already had a full quota of foreign teachers mainly from North America. However, no one took it upon themselves to advise me of the reality of this situation for fear of losing face. Blissfully unaware of my rejection, I laboured under the misapprehension that I was a member of the university staff and spent ten days waiting to be given my timetable of classes. Meanwhile the university authorities were regarding me as a paying guest who was racking up his bills for board and lodgings. This misunderstanding was not the auspicious start I had hoped for.

I am by nature a very lucky person. Or maybe it is simply because I am optimistic by nature that luck seems to come my way. Anyway, a nearby college heard that there was an English teacher surplus to requirements and came in to make an offer for my services. Professor Han, the head of the English Department of Shenyang Pharmaceutical University, came to see me and offered me the job of English teacher. He was delighted to find that, unlike the majority of foreigners teaching English in China, I was a qualified teacher and had a degree in languages.

I went to give the place a look over. It was much smaller, only two thousand students as opposed to twelve thousand, but I would be in the unique position of being the only English teacher. From the point of view of improving my Chinese, this appealed to me as I would not be surrounded by a lot of English-speaking foreigners. The living conditions too were far superior. Instead of the one room at the Northeast University, I would enjoy the status of a foreign expert and have a suite of five rooms including my own kitchen and bathroom. Pretty good. I was still rather reluctant to leave as I had already made quite a few Chinese and foreign friends but I knew in my heart that I had to leave and this was as good an offer as I was likely to receive. And so I went. I could't have imagined how lucky I was. Shenyang Pharmaceutical University is one of only two such elite establishments in the whole of China, the other being in Nanjing. Founded in 1931 as the School of Military Surgeons for the Red Army, it was now at the forefront of research and development into new drugs. The intake of students was of the highest calibre and their standard of written and spoken English was outstanding. Not only that, but although I did not know it at the time, my future wife was a fellow teacher and student in my postgraduate English class. The motto of the university was "Be united and diligent. Be practical and dedicated." I heartily concurred with all these exhortations. I just added one of my own, "Be lucky."

On the morning of Saturday the 12th of May, Li Yu Min, my contact at the Liaoning Province Physical Culture Commission, telephoned to tell me that he would bring the tai chi teacher they had assigned to me. He or was it she , I didn't know, was called Liu You Zhen. In fact, teacher Liu was a lady and a very special and important lady at that.

Liu You Zhen was the Senior Coach of the Liaoning Province Wushu Team and as such was one of the top coaches in the North-East of China. She was a small, quiet, reserved woman with short black cropped hair and gave very little away in her manner and facial expressions. She was forty nine years old and came originally from Ba County in Hebei Province. Her teacher had been one of the most famous martial artists in China at that time - Li Wen Zhen. In 1957 at the age of 17, she had taken first prize at the Chinese National Martial Arts Conference. As a teacher she had visited Japan, Burma, Pakistan and Korea. Since 1972 she had become a Liaoning Province Wushu Team coach and was now the senior coach. She had trained many national martial arts champions, such as Zhang Shao Yi, Liu Qing Hua and Yu Miao. Among these, Zhang Shao Yi was the all-round Chinese ladies national champion and first World Martial Arts all-round ladies champion. And now she was about to coach me, a forty-one year old tai chi teacher from England who was all-round champion of ..... well nothing yet actually. I felt immensely privileged and rather daunted to be assigned one of the senior coaches in the province. I surmised that as far as my hosts were concerned it was a question of "face". The Liaoning Sports Commissions could not give me, their honoured foreign guest, just any old teacher. It had to be the best. This rather placed on me the burden of responsibility to be an outstanding student. I would try.

I had intimated to the Sports Commissions that I wished to study Yang style tai chi. The proposal was that Coach Liu would first of all revise the 24 and 48 step routines with me before teaching me the newly devised Yang style 40 forms routine. I would have preferred to learn traditional Yang style but I was only too happy to accept what I was being offered. I would meet my teacher for three one-hour lessons a week on Tuesday, Thursday and Saturday afternoons. She lived nearby at the Shenyang Academy of Music where her husband, Zhao Yue Chao, was a flute teacher. We arranged to meet the following Tuesday at 2 o'clock in Nan Hu Park. Sports coaches, especially at the highest level, have to be experts in and judges of the standard routines of every martial art tested and examined at championship level. From the age of five, Liu You Zhen had practised changchuan, nanchuan, shaolinchuan, sword, broadsword, staff, spear and many other external disciplines. In addition she had learned tai chi, bagua and xing yi among the internal arts. If I had been worried that she might be a Jack of All Trades and Master of None, I need not have worried at all. In fact she was a master of them all. As I met more and more high level coaches in China, I never ceased to be amazed at how many forms and routines from how many disciplines they could remember. And how easily they were able to switch from one to another. I supposed that if I had been brought up in China from the age of five and had spent my formative, impressionable teenage years learning and practising for five hours or more a day, then I too would possess such skills.

As a Senior Wushu Coach, Liu You Zhen's entire mentality and training schedule were geared to preparing young, fit, highly-trained, receptive and motivated students for participation in top level national competitions. In her eyes, I was no different. She didn't seem to see that I was a middle-aged, unfit, basically trained, stiff and awkward left-hander who was out of his depth. No one could question my motivation or my receptiveness within the confines of my Chinese language ability. But I was fundamentally an amateur in both senses of the word, in that I engaged in tai chi as a pastime and that I loved the art that I practised. She on the other hand was a thorough professional in the world of professionals. She was used to dealing with national champions and as such would not tolerate mediocrity. This mild-mannered, quietly-spoken lady of around fifty years of age was actually a ruthless coaching machine who didn't suffer fools gladly. I loved her.

As arranged at the weekend we met at the gate of Nan Hu Park on Tuesday afternoon for our first lesson. I ran through the 24 forms and 48 forms routines as far as I had been taught. She asked who had taught me and when I replied Professor Pang, head of physical education from the Fuxin Mining Institute, she snorted disdainfully and told me in no uncertain terms that I had been incorrectly taught and that there were basic flaws in my forms. She proceeded to dissect my performance movement by movement, posture by posture until my tai chi lay like a dead carcass on the floor. My first instinct was to defend my former teacher but then I remembered the words of Coaches Luan and Yao whom I had met in Shenyang on my first visit the previous year. They had said that there weren't any good tai chi teachers in a backwater like Fuxin. Maybe they had been right after all. They hadn't been arrogant but simply realistic. Of course, it was all a question of relativity. As far as they were concerned, their standards were so high that almost anything short of perfect was inferior. I bit my tongue and said nothing. I was preparing to be humiliated and to *Chi Ku* - taste bitterness - once more. Before leaving she asked me to show her the 32 sword form routine. This time she appeared to be more satisfied although she did annoyingly suck her teeth from time to time. At the conclusion, she simply said "*Bu cuo*" (Pretty good), got on her bike and rode off, leaving my reputation and that of Professor Pang at least slightly redeemed.

I must admit that I felt guilty about taking up so much of Coach Liu's valuable time. Although it was only three hours a week, I was sure that the interruptions to see me ate annoyingly into her weekly schedule. She had the provincial squad to coach and meetings to attend as well as carrying on the normal functions of her family life. Stoically she never complained. I would have felt happier if I had been paying for her services but Li Yu Min from the Liaoning Sports Commission reassured me that payment was out of the question as I was their sponsored guest. I wanted to broach the subject with Liu You Zhen herself but simply felt too embarrassed. I just hoped that by being a model student she wouldn't secretly resent me for taking advantage of her time and services. After a while, it was patently obvious to me that she had not volunteered to teach me tai chi but that she had been commandeered by her superiors at the Sports Commission to carry out the thankless task of teaching elementary tai chi skills to a foreigner. She was not in a position to say "No". Neither could I refuse the offer to be taught by a senior coach which the Sports Commission had put at my disposal. After a few weeks, Coach Liu asked me if I wouldn't mind moving our classes to 5:30 in the evening which was just before dinner time. I was only too willing to oblige. Occasionally she would telephone me in the morning and ask if I wouldn't mind cancelling the class that day as she had something more important to attend to. I was only too happy to go along with these concessions in the hope that the time we did spend together would be productive and instructional. And indeed it was.

Having revised the 24 and 48 form routines, we began in earnest on the Yang style competition form. Having practised the traditional 108 Yang style form for nearly ten years, I was familiar with many of the movements but they were performed differently and out of sequences. Effectively I was learning from scratch. It seemed that with every new teacher, I had to begin again at the very beginning. Liu You Zhen was an excellent teacher though to my mind a little lacking in patience. Of course, she was used to high calibre wushu athletes who picked up on her meaning immediately. I was a naturally slow learner with a basic command of Chinese who liked to take things one step at a time. She would sometimes show her frustration with me and be ruthlessly critical if I could't get something right. It was while training alongside her that I really witnessed for the first time the difference between the internal and the external content of tai chi. I would assiduously follow her movements in Grasping the Bird's Tail - ward off, roll back, press and push. My movements were identical to hers but they just weren't the same. At rest, Liu You Zhen was a short, rather dumpy and static figure. However, in practice, her body was so relaxed, supple and fluid. It possessed a liquid quality. Her movements, like mine, were circular. But there were circles within her circles and energy was clearly radiating from within. What energy I possessed was principally on the surface. I realized that she was pointing me in the right direction by constantly emphasizing *Song Yao* (**松腰**) - Relax the waist. However, at this stage no matter how much I tried, I simply could not emulate the looseness and softness of her body and the relaxation in particular of her waist. It was a case of the spirit being willing but the flesh weak. I realized what was required but my body as yet did not possess the qualities to follow my intentions. The learning and correction process is based on the assumption that one can make immediate adjustments. This simply was not possible with tai chi. It was not a case of lack of understanding or lack of willingness on my part, but simply the gulf between her level and mine was too wide to cross in one step. It was a case of transition - taking one small step at a time.The problem for me was how to bridge the gap between my level and hers. I did the only thing I could - practise, practise and still more practise. Fortunately my teaching schedule was extremely light, only twelve hours a week. This was quite normal for a foreign teacher. The Chinese teachers themselves sometimes only taught as little as six hours a week. Anyway this left me plenty of time for practising. Looking back now, I realise that this was exactly what I should have done and accounts for the softness of my movements now - something which I have never lost. From time to time, Liu You Zhen was absent. For two weeks in July she went off to attend the National Wushu Championships and then in November she went to Nanjing for a fortnight. Gradually by the end of the year our three classes had been reduced to two. I realised long before this that our association was petering out and was doomed not to be an entirely fruitful and productive teacher-student relationship right from the very start.

In mid-January 1991 at the time of the Chinese Spring Festival, I flew home to England for an intended two weeks holiday. On my first weekend back, I was a passenger in a very nasty road accident. My friends and I were returning from a Chinese meal in Manchester's Chinatown when the car skidded at fifty miles an hour, somersaulted and hit a tree. As the car crumpled and the doors burst open, myself and another rear seat passenger were thrown out. She was severely injured. She broke her leg, her pelvis, her arm and her jaw as well as suffering internal injuries to her organs. I cracked a couple of ribs. Maybe you could say I was lucky. But I remember that as the crash was about to happen, I slowed everything down, concentrated on making my body very soft and remained conscious throughout. Everyone else blacked out and lost consciousness till the ambulances appeared on the scene. I believe the fact that I emerged relatively unscathed from what could easily have been a fatal accident was down to my tai chi and *Qigong* training in China. In this instance, tai chi really was good for my health.

On my delayed return to China my college was very sympathetic and eased me back into my teaching. I telephoned Liu You Zhen and told her what had happened. She could't have been more sympathetic. Although I had not suffered any serious injuries, my body was still extremely stiff and sore and my ribs gave me considerable pain. We agreed not to continue our tai chi classes for the time being. I have to admit that I wasn't too distressed as I did not relish continuing to be a burden around Liu You Zhen's neck. It seemed that fate had stepped in once more to change the direction of my tai chi journey. I did see Coach Liu on a couple more occasions that year but we both knew it was over. Besides, by this time I had made other arrangements for my tai chi education.

THE SHENYANG INSTITUTE OF PHYSICAL CULTURE

Shenyang is the fourth largest city in China after Shanghai, Beijing and Tianjin. It is also the home of one of the six premier Institutes of Physical Culture in China, the others being in Beijing, Shanghai, Chengdu, Wuhan and Xian. It is the largest advanced Sports Institute in North-East China and comes directly under the auspices of the Chinese National Sports Commission. It is possible to study traditional Chinese sports as well as western team games. These range from table-tennis and gymnastics to football and basketball, from speedskating to track and field. And of course there is wushu - Chinese martial arts - from changchuan and nanchuan to shaolinchuan and tanglangchuan, from sword and broadsword to staff and spear. And the internal arts from xingyichuan and baguazhang to tai chi chuan.

The Institute is situated in the north of the city in the Huanggu District just to the east of the perimeter road running around the vast expanses of Beiling Park. From May 1990 until August 1991 I taught English at the Pharmaceutical University in the south of the city near Nan Hu Park. It was a good forty-five minutes cycle ride between the two places. And yet I made this round trip three times a week to study with my tai chi coaches. All this changed when I returned to China in December 1991. I was offered the job as the Institute's resident English teacher in a reciprocal agreement whereby I received free full-time martial arts tuition in return. I stayed there until May 1993 during which time I graduated from the Institute in Chinese internal arts and was commissioned to write the definitive English language handbook for Chinese Olympic sports coaches by the Chinese National Sports Commission.

For the moment, let's return to the very beginning. In 1989 I had been made aware of the existence of these elite Institutes when I tried to plan my return to China after June the 4th. I had written to Beijing and Shanghai but either their courses were too short or too expensive, and so I had overlooked this option. Once back in Shenyang I decided to take matters into my own hands and contact the Foreign Affairs Office of the Shenyang Institute. It was much easier to deal with these matters personally now I was on the spot.

There were several advantages to finding a high level tai chi coach in this way. Principally, I would be the master of my own destiny. Previously I had been the sponsored guest of the Liaoning People's Association for Friendship with Foreign Countries and more recently the Liaoning Province Physical Culture Commission. On both occasions, my teachers had been assigned to me whether they liked it or not, and as far as I knew had not received any additional payment for their inconvenience. Whilst they undoubtedly gave me their undivided attention and the best possible instruction, I couldn't help but feel uneasy that they did not fulfil the duty of teaching a foreign tai chi student willingly. However, by going to a Sports Institute and enrolling on a course or hiring the services of a coach, I would be more in control of the situation. I could pay for any instruction I received on an hourly basis. I could choose what I wanted to learn in terms of styles and forms. I could study more deeply and more widely. This approach to finding a compatible tai chi teacher struck me as being more satisfactory to both sides.

On Saturday the 26th of May 1990 I cycled up to the Shenyang Sports Institute arriving at 9 a.m. At first the gatekeeper was reluctant to let me in as I had no credentials or letter of introduction to show him. Eventually I managed to smooth-talk my way onto the campus and was directed to the block where all the offices were located. Up on the second floor I found the Foreign Affairs Office and its Director, Zhang Huo Ran. I managed to make my meaning understood but he still preferred to call in an English-speaking interpreter to carry out our negotiations. A few minutes later after I had sunk myself into his plush leather armchair and sipped a mug of his jasmine tea, in walked a diminutive young lady wearing black horn-rimmed glasses and sporting a *Wu hao tou* (a number five haircut) popular amongst girls at that time. She was very cute. She smiled at me and with the slightest trace of an American-English accent said, "Hello, I'm Wendy." Her real name turned out to be Wen Hui, one of the young English teachers on the campus. I was immediately impressed with her near-perfect English and we established an instant rapport. She had a lovely smile, an infectious girlish laugh and a twinkle in her eye. She struck me as being a very smart young lady. I trusted her to help me.

Wherever you went in China, people liked to be paid in dollars. It was a strong currency and on the black market could be exchanged well over the odds for Chinese currency. I remembered that the Beijing Institute charged its fees in dollars, between 2,500 and 5,000 for a year's tuition. Director Zhang was looking at me far too amiably for my liking. I could swear I saw dollar signs light up in his eyes when he looked at me. Through Wen Hui he told me that it would cost me 250 dollars a month for tuition, board and lodging. I first of all explained to him that I was already employed in another university in Shenyang which supplied me with meals and accommodation. Moreover, I was British and not American and so did not carry US dollars. I had a resident permit and a work permit and was paid in the Chinese currency of *Renminbi*. I don't think Director Zhang was too pleased. Wen Hui was doing her best to keep a straight face but couldn't help the slightest giggle from escaping . Director Zhang tried another tack. He quickly converted a hundred US dollars into Renminbi. Wen Hui translated "Will you pay this amount for a month's tuition alone?" I shook my head and told her that it was more than my monthly Chinese salary. The Chinese love to bargain. You should never stop bargaining until you reach about a third of the original asking price. English people are too embarrassed to bargain. They prefer just to pay the price. The reality was that I had to bargain as I simply didn't have the kind of money he was asking for. "How many hours a week do you want to train?" Director Zhang asked me. I explained that I had to fit my training in with my English teaching. I decided that I needed to train three times a week on Tuesday, Thursday and Saturday morning. "Six hours a week," I replied. "Why not make it nine?" asked Zhang. "Three hours is better than two." I thought it over. "Alright. Three hours on Tuesday and Saturday mornings and two hours on Thursday. Eight hours a week. How much will you charge me an hour?" "Fifteen yuan," he replied. "Ten," I said. "Twelve," he retorted. "OK. Done." I agreed. Director Zhang multiplied the figures out. "Eight times twelve, that's ninety six. Let's call it a hundred, shall we?" I let him have the last word and we shook hands on the deal. Once outside the office, Wen Hui couldn't stop herself from giggling uncontrollably and clapping her hands with glee. "That was very good," she said, "but you didn't tell him what you wanted to study or with whom." I clapped my hand to my forehead. I had been so preoccupied with making all the financial arrangements that I had completely forgotten about my main priority - the tai chi. We turned around and headed back to the office. Director Zhang was on the phone. Wen Hui explained to him our omission and he asked me what I wanted to learn. In a flash I replied "Chen style tai chi." Zhang nodded, rubbed his chin and said "Guan laoshi." I looked at Wen Hui for approval of his choice of teacher. She smiled and nodded. "When do we start?" I asked. "Next Tuesday morning. Alright." Now it really was settled.

Wen Hui invited me back to her place for tea and eventually lunch when I met her husband, Qi Zuo Cheng, who was a track and field coach at the Institute. They lived in a minute, one-roomed flat in the teachers' accommodation block next to the tennis courts. I told Wen Hui that her English was very good. This was explained by the fact that she had graduated from the Dalian Foreign Language Institute which was one of the top language schools in the North of China. All the teachers were Americans. Hence her American accent. I also found out that she had an interest in wushu. As a teenager she had been a member of the Liaoning Province junior wushu team. She came from a sporting background as her father was a provincial and national weightlifting coach, and her brother was a junior weightlifting champion. She looked like a pocket Hercules herself. In view of our shared interests and the fact that we were getting on so well, I asked her if she would be free to attend any of my classes. Fortunately most of her lessons were in the afternoon so she agreed to pop into my first class the following Tuesday morning from 8 till 11. She knew some tai chi but didn't know any Chen style. In fact she was curious about why I had chosen to learn Chen style at all. I told her about my previous visit to Shenyang in 1989 when I had met coaches Luan and Yao from the Liaoning Wushu Team and the Liaoning Sports Technique Institute and they had given me a performance of Chen style which had made such a deep impression on me. I was a little worried about Director Zhang palming me off with any old teacher but Wen Hui's nod had reassured me. "Is coach Guan any good?" "Oh, yes," replied Wen Hui. "He's the best. You can ask anyone. He's definitely the best." At the time I just accepted her stamp of approval. It was only later that I came to realise that she had actually meant what she said. He really was the best, the best allround coach I ever met in China. I consider it a privilege to have been taught by him.

Wen Hui asked me what I would like for lunch. "*Qiezi*" (eggplant) I replied. While her husband Qi Zuo Cheng cooked for us on the communal facilities in the corridor outside their flat, we carried on our conversation. She was a very ambitious young lady who planned to go abroad to study. The Institute had sent several coaches to Belgium with which they had a special relationship.However, they seemed to be under the delusion that everyone in Europe spoke English. When I told Wen Hui that actually they spoke French among several other languages in Belgium, she was most upset. I told her not to worry as I had a degree in French and German and would be only too pleased to teach her. At this news she perked up no end. I am pleased to report that Wen Hui has now settled in Belgium. She not only speaks French but also Flemish and Dutch. What is more, she is currently the Belgian national ladies tai chi champion.

As we were about to have lunch, there was a knock at the door. In came a rather rotund, robust, ruddy-faced chap who appeared to be out of breath. He was a man in his late fifties with a blustery disposition who seemed to carry his own ball of energy around with him, such was his animated personality. Wen Hui introduced us. He turned out to be Li Le Zheng, one of the senior vice-presidents of the Institute. What was more, he loved to speak English and my presence was actually very lucky for him. The following week he was acting as the Chairman of an international sports conference in Beijing attended by delegations from all over the world and needed to make the opening address in English. He was self-taught and spoke quite good English himself as well as being fluent in Russian. He wanted to ask Wen Hui to run through his speech for him to ensure that there weren't any serious mistakes. I gladly agreed to help. He was delighted. And when Wen Hui told President Li that I was coming to study at the Institute, he was even more delighted. He was a real anglophile, read English voraciously and always listened to the BBC World Service on his short-wave radio. The warmth and charm of this man were completely overwhelming. I came to see him as my surrogate father in China and we eventually collaborated to write a book together for the Chinese National Sports Commission.

Li Le Zheng walked me around the campus before I left. After continuing our conversation in his office, we returned to see Director Zhang at the Foreign Affairs Office. President Li made a point of emphasizing that I should be given the best treatment and instruction that the Institute could offer. It was nice to have friends in high places. He too seemed to approve of the choice of Coach Guan as my teacher. I couldn't ask for any more. President Li was extremely proud of the Shenyang Institute, was keen to promote it abroad and to attract more foreign students. Maybe it wasn't as famous as Beijing or Shanghai but it could boast among its students national champions, Asian champions and even world champions in their respective sports. Not only that but the coaches were of the highest calibre, many of them being former Chinese national champions themselves. The coaches were also in great demand abroad in such countries as Russia and Japan. This outgoing policy reflected the gregarious nature of Li Le Zheng himself. Although he didn't look much of a sportsman as he puffed his way around the campus on his bike, he had a very competitive disposition and sporting spirit. As we passed the athletics running track, he pointed out the building which housed the wushu training hall on the right so that I would know where to come for my first class the following Tuesday. I wished him good luck for his conference in Beijing as he saw me off at the main gate. This time the gatekeeper smiled and waved at me. He would remember me next time.

I cycled back home, well pleased with my morning's work. I earned 800 yuan a month. The teachers at my university and presumably the coaches at the Institute too only earned about 200 to 250 yuan a month, a quarter of my foreign expert's salary. It seemed a pitiful amount. I would have to spend half of my salary on my tuition fees but I considered it value for money. Translated into English terms it was only about a pound an hour which was ludicrously cheap for the services of a top sports coach. I couldn't wait to begin.

I wasn't too sure what to expect as I waited in the *wushuguan* - the martial arts training hall - just before eight o'clock in the morning on Tuesday the 5th of June 1991. I supposed that if Guan was an experienced senior coach as I had been led to believe, he would be in his fifties and perhaps rather strict and serious. The massive parquet-floored training hall was deserted at that time of day. Wushu squad training didn't start until 9 or half past. I had a three hour lesson ahead of me. I hoped my Chinese would last out, that we would get on well and that there would be a productive student-teacher relationship. I felt a little nervous and hoped that Wen Hui would be on time to introduce us and break the ice. It was still only five minutes to eight. There was a bank of full length mirrors at the far end of the hall. I went down and began to practise my forms in front of them.

I didn't notice as the swing doors opened quietly on the stroke of eight and a shadowy figure slipped into the hall. It was only when I looked in the mirror as I finished my form that I realised he was standing behind me. He almost looked like my reflection. We were both wearing white T-shirts and track suit bottoms. We were of the same height and build and looked about the same age. We could have been brothers except for the fact that one of us was English and one of us was Chinese. "Hello," he said. "My name is Guan Tie Yun." I was rather taken aback by this as I hadn't expected him to speak English. "*Ni hui shuo yingyu*?" (You can speak English?) I said. He placed the thumb and index finger of his right hand close together and said, "A little." The fact that Coach Guan spoke English was an unexpected bonus. In fact his English wasn't at all bad. It was about the same as my Chinese. So there didn't seem to be any problem with communication between us. However, he did strike me as being rather quiet and shy. There again I was somewhat introverted by nature and felt quite comfortable in his company. He asked me all the standard questions that Chinese people ask. Where do you come from? What do you do for a living? How many children do you have? How old are you? Chinese people never ask you whether you are married or not. They assume that everyone is married, as in China it is highly unusual for someone not to be married. He was surprised when I told him that I was forty-one and still single. By coincidence he was forty-one, too. "When is your birthday?" he asked. "The fourth of December. How about you?" I asked. "The eighth of December," he replied with a shy smile. "That makes me your older brother by four days," I said. We were both born in 1948, the year of the rat so that meant we were both born under the same sign. Quite a coincidence. I told him that I was a full-time teacher of tai chi in England. He seemed impressed. I think he liked me.

At this moment Wen Hui turned up. "Sorry I'm late," she said. "I can see you two have already met." They addressed each other as "*Laoshi*" which means teacher and is the polite form of address among fellow professionals. I asked Guan, "*Wo zenme chenghu ni*?" (How should I address you?) "*Guan laoshi*," he replied. I told him to call me Howard but he often slipped back into the Chinese version of my surname "*Tuo Ma Si*." So, what next? The polite introductions had been made. The social niceties had been observed. I expected Guan to give me a demonstration of Chen style as Coach Luan had done and for us then to learn four or five movements of the form. That is what my previous teachers had done. But not him. He gave me a history lesson on the origins of Chen style tai chi from the founder, Chen Wang Ting, the development of Chenjiagou, the Chen Village in Henan Province, and the division of the style into two branches - Old Style and New Style. He gave me an analysis of the two traditional long forms *Yi Lu* and *Er Lu* which was also known as *Pao Cui*. The latter was unique in tai chi in that it retained the fast, pounding, stamping and jumping elements. He explained some of the characteristics of Chen style such as *Fa Jin*, the sudden release of explosive energy which accompanied certain movements, and *Chan Si Jin*, reeling silk energy. Chen style was characterised by its spiralling and twisting external movements and the energy which also travelled internally in a spiral fashion. He took up a low posture and repeated the same Chen movements several times. He then asked me to put my arms tightly around his waist from behind. He performed the same movement again and as he released the energy I couldn't help but relinquish my grasp and fairly flew backwards, such was the extent of his *Fa Jin*. I found that Guan was extremely methodical and systematic at making his points and always illustrated them with a practical demonstration.

The traditional long Chen forms contained 83 and 71 movements respectively and were too long for a novice such as myself to learn. Short forms did exist. Chen Xiao Wang, grandson of Chen Fa Ke had devised a 38 movement set and another tai chi expert had created a 36 movement set. Guan Tie Yun had decided to teach me the 56 step international championship routine which was a combination of the two traditional long forms. It was the standard Chen style form examined in national and international competitions. I had already learned the Yang style 40 competition routine from Liu You Zhen so I was familiar with the format. Guan had learned the form in Beijing from Kan Gui Xiang who was responsible for developing the routine. Guan informed me that he also knew both traditional long forms. As a student he had studied for a year at the Shanghai Institute under Chuan Sui Tang, a student of the famous Master, Zhu Tian Cai from Henan Province. He never boasted about anything and simply told me things in a very matter of fact kind of way. He just felt that it was important that I should know certain facts. I felt frustrated sometimes when teachers weren't forthcoming with information or explanations. This criticism could never be levelled at Guan Tie Yun. He was always completely open with me.

By this time it was nearly half past nine and I still hadn't done any actual tai chi. However, I had made a lot of notes and learned a great deal. It was obvious that Guan was highly intelligent and extremely knowledgeable as well as being a skilful exponent of martial arts. At least I assumed he was. The wushu team had arrived and were being drilled in their *Jibengong*, basic warm-up techniques, on the other side of the training hall. I noted them glancing over curiously in my direction and smiled back at them. Then I realised that they weren't only watching me, but they were also watching Coach Guan. After some further discussion, he told me to "*Xiu xi yi huir*" - take a rest, and asked me to pay attention and watch carefully. He was going to give me a performance of the Chen style competition form. He instructed me to take note of all the points we had discussed as they were applied in practice in the form. As soon as he began, a hush fell over the wushu training hall as the students stopped what they were doing and watched Guan's performance. I recognised the routine as the one demonstrated by Luan Xiao Yan, but whereas Luan's was spectacular, Guan's was positively scintillating. As I watched I felt the hairs stand up on the back of my neck and I had goosepimples, so breathtaking was the display of tremendous technique, rhythm, energy, concentration and sheer power. It was awesome. At the final movement, Buddha's Warrior Attendant Pounds the Mortar, the whole place seemed to shake and reverberate with the stamping power and then there was a tremendous sense of calm. I had almost forgotten to take a breath during the performance and was left gasping for air, whereas Guan seemed perfectly relaxed and at ease.

The students returned to their basic technique and Guan came to join me and Wen Hui. I wanted to say, "That was brilliant" but I felt that he was an extremely modest man who would only have been embarrassed by praise. I asked him how he managed to remain so relaxed and in control of what was obviously a very physically and mentally demanding routine. He was barely out of breath after his exertions. He replied that it was important to be in control of the internal energy and not let the energy control you. As a student when he first started practising Chen style he had been left exhausted and mentally worn out until his teacher taught him how to relax and breathe correctly. The phrase "*Fang Song*," Relax, was the most frequently used by all my teachers. Guan was no exception.

Finally Guan said, "Let's practise a little." But it still wasn't the beginning of the form and it wasn't a complete technique. He made Wen Hui and me stand in a horse stance with our backs straight and our legs perfectly arched. Then following him we had to sink in the stance, take the weight entirely into the right leg and draw the left leg up slowly beside the right. Next with the ankle turned inwards we had to slide out sideways on the heel of the left foot and extend the left leg while still keeping the weight in the right. This Chen style technique of stepping was called *Ca* which means wipe or rub. Then we had to gradually transfer the weight into the middle to form another horse stance with the legs perfectly bowed and the feet parallel. Facing the full length mirrors repeating this technique, we progressed sideways to the left then all the way back to the right. We did this single technique for about half an hour. "*Lei bu lei*?" (Are you tired?) Guan asked us. I shook my head but I thought Wen Hui had had enough and I didn't think I would be able to walk properly for a week, let alone cycle all the way back home. I felt and looked like a saddle-sore cowboy. Eventually Guan called time. He opened his folder and took out four sheets of paper on which he had neatly written the names of the entire movements of the form in both Chinese, Pinyin and English. "I thought you would like to learn these," he said, "before you start learning the form." I thanked him. "Don't forget to practise what I have taught you," he continued, "and please relax. See you next time." With these parting words, he picked up his things and left the training hall. Wen Hui looked at me and asked knowingly "Well what do you think? Have you learned anything?" "More than you can imagine," I replied. "More than you can imagine."

Guan Tie Yun was not very forthcoming about himself. Most of what I learned about him was from Wen Hui, President Li and the other students and teachers. He was a very shy, modest, retiring man and extremely reticent about his past and his achievements. He had graduated from the Shenyang Institute and had also spent a year studying at the Shanghai Institute. He was an expert in many disciplines of the martial arts both ancient and modern. Although what he taught nowadays consisted solely of modern competition routines, he was at heart a traditionalist and had studied with traditional masters particularly in the fields of tai chi, bagua, tongbeiquan , huaquan and yuanyangquan. In 1983 he was the Liaoning Province allround champion in traditional wushu. At a very early age he qualified as a Chinese national wushu referee. He was a specialist and leading national authority on several traditional arts. For someone so young he was also something of a scholar. He had written several books notably on tongbeiquan and Chinese freefighting techniques. He was a major contributor of over one hundred articles to the definitive work "The Chinese Dictionary of Wushu." In collaboration with three other coaches/masters he was the author of the standard million word reference book "A Complete Record of Chinese Wushu." Not a bad C.V.

If Guan was such a high calibre coach, I wondered how come he had so much spare time to teach me. I expected his time to be at a premium. He was obviously a great asset to the Institute. As I gradually discovered, his talents were severely underused. Most members of the team only studied the modern wushu competition routines and whilst I was there, no student showed an interest in tai chi or tai chi sword. They all preferred the fast external styles. Guan did teach the general students 24 step tai chi and basic changquan. I considered this a terrible and demeaning waste of his talents. Not only the students but all the other teachers admired and respected him greatly. He was held up by the Institute authorities as a model coach whose dedication, knowledge and teaching methods should be followed and duplicated. And yet Coach Guan was a more useful asset abroad than he was at home in China. He had already spent six months in the city of Kyoto in Japan where he had taught shaolinchuan and Chen style tai chi. They absolutely adored him in Japan and constantly invited him to return. In fact the Institute sent many of its best coaches abroad to earn welcome foreign revenue. Coach of the Institute's men's wushu team, Lu Yong Xiang, spent so much time in Russia that he was eventually appointed head coach of the Russian National Wushu Team. Of course I wasn't going to complain about the fact that Guan was so underused and consequently had so much time to teach me. In fact he was delighted that a foreigner especially was interested enough to make the trip to China to learn traditional martial arts. He thought I was very brave. I thought I was rather lucky. The other students' loss was my gain.

My classes continued on Tuesday, Thursday and Saturday mornings. On Thursdays I only trained for two hours from 9:30 till 11:30. Each time after training I usually had lunch with Wen Hui and her husband before cycling back to the university to give my lessons in the afternoon. Fortunately in China they tend to take an extended lunch break from 11:30 till about 2. This allows them not only enough time to eat but also to have a midday nap, an essential element of Chinese everyday life.

By now I was becoming quite familiar with Guan Tie Yun. I began to wonder about the other members of staff in the wushu department and the young students in the Institute wushu team. It was quite a small department, headed by the fearsome Professor Mu Xiu Jie. Not only the students but also the teachers were quite frightened of her. Although quite small and unassuming, she ruled the wushu training hall with a rod of iron. Later she was to coach me but for the moment I only observed her tongue-lashings from a distance. The standards she set were very high and woe betide anyone who fell below them. I sometimes saw the teachers crying after Mu had verbally laid into them. And that was only the men! However, she did have a soft spot for Guan Tie Yun and he was clearly her favourite. As Guan's private student, I was able to bask a little in his limelight.

The first week of training followed a familiar pattern. Guan liked to talk, explain and clarify before we actually did anything. This was contrary to my previous teachers' approach of launching themselves immediately into the form with little or no preparatory ground work and explanation. He was equally at home in English or Chinese and actively encouraged me to speak English to him so that he could practise his oral skills. I liked the idea of us both being students and teachers simultaneously. It put us both at our ease. I always came armed with a pen, a notebook and a dictionary. He was insistent that everything was crystal clear in my mind before going on. His approach was systematic and meticulous. It was easy to see why the students admired him so much and his fellow teachers modelled their teaching methods on his. I was determined to show him that I was a model student through my dedication, application and practice.

An opportunity arose to demonstrate precisely this. In the early summer months in Shenyang, from time to time we were subjected to sudden and torrential downpours which left the roads and the low-lying buildings flooded. One Saturday morning in June fell victim to such a downpour. Undeterred I set off from the Pharmaceutical University at around 6.30 a.m. for my morning class at the Institute. As I cycled north past Qingnian Park, the water level was already about a foot deep.The further north I went, the worse it got. By the time I reached Chongshan Road, it was impassable to vehicular traffic. At this stage, it would have been easier to turn round and go home than to press on to my destination. I was wearing a rain cape but by now my lower body was completely soaked as the water was washing up around my chain guard. I was determined not to give up, driven on by my desire not to miss my lesson with Guan Tie Yun. Eventually it was impossible to pedal any more. I dismounted and pushed my bike up the road to the east gate of the Institute. I paused outside Guan's block of flats. It was totally surrounded by water which was lapping up the steps between the ground and first floors. Hauling my bike onto my back,I sloshed through the thigh-deep water, entered the building and went up to the second floor. Guan answered. His face was a picture. "I didn't think you'd come. I wasn't expecting you," he said. "Are you mad?" "I didn't want to miss our lesson," I confessed. I must have looked a pathetic sight - soaked from head to foot, muddy and bedraggled but I had made my point. I had braved all the elements rather than sacrifice our class. That morning we held our session in his parlour in front of a warm fire. I steamed throughout the entire three hours. Guan always took me seriously after that.

We spent a lot of time practising basic elements - stances, steps, hand and arm techniques. He concentrated especially on the spiralling character of movements particular to Chen style tai chi. Usually in a low horse stance we practised techniques in isolation from the form. In fact we didn't touch the form itself during our first week. We repeatedly practised such hand techniques as The Fist of Covering Hands and Arm, Cloud Hands and Step Back and Whirl Arms on Both Sides. I suppose at first that I was frustrated by Guan's approach as I couldn't wait to learn the form, but I remained patient. In the middle of the second week, we actually started on the routine proper but only learned two movements, Commencing Form and Buddha's Warrior Attendant Pounds Mortar-Right Style. Guan spent an eternity on the opening movement, the breathing and the description of the circles with the hands. He stressed the initiation of movement from the waist. When I didn't quite get it right, he held my waist with his hands and tried to guide me, then he repeated the movement several times himself with me holding him by the waist. This was also the first time there had been physical contact with any of my teachers. Guan was quite a shy, demure person but he was also very tactile and intimate when necessary which was quite unusual among Chinese people. He stressed the co-ordination of the hand and leg movements with the waist acting as the axis. When we came to the movement involving the fist pounding down on the uplifted palm and the simultaneous stamping with the right foot, I was preparing to slam down with all my might when he stopped me in full flow. "What did I tell you," he said. "Relax and don't forget to breathe." I then realised that my shoulders were tense, I was holding my breath and I was just concentrating on using brute external force. "Wind up the *Chan Si Jin* - spiralling internal energy from your *Dan Tian*," he said, "and just release it when you feel the time is right." "*Yong Yi Bu Yong Li.*" (用意不用力) - Use the mind. Do not use force. Guan was very fond of using the traditional wushu idioms to make his point. I later found this to be one of Yang Cheng Fu's ten essential points for the practice of tai chi. I listened to his advice, listened to my body, listened to my mind and found that it worked.

The notebook that I carried to my classes was beginning to fill up quickly with words, phrases and idioms. Patterns began to emerge which told me a lot about Guan's methods of teaching. Firstly, there were words such as *Zhou* meaning axis, *Zhidian* meaning pivot/fulcrum and *Jiezou* meaning rhythm. This underlying theme of technical language illustrated Guan's preoccupation with body mechanics. Secondly, I found a whole series of words, ending in *Fa* which means method or way of doing something. There was the word *Fangfa* itself meaning method followed by *Shou fa*, *Shenfa*, *Bufa* and *Yanfa* which literally mean hand method, body method, stepping method and eye method. This displayed his attention to detail in every part of the body being actively involved. In addition to the above, was the word *Yongfa* which means use or practical application. Every movement was learned in the context of the form and how it might be used in a martial role.There was a method, a skill, a technique an application and an art in perfecting any movement or posture. However physically difficult or complex a movement was, he assured me that I would be able to do it if I paid attention to and closely followed his methods. Thirdly, I noticed his love of idioms in order to concisely make a point. Some of these were Yang Cheng Fu's essential points such as *Chen Jian Zhui Zhou* (沉肩坠肘) - Sink the shoulders, drop the elbows and *Song Kua Yuan Dang* (松腰圆裆) - Relax the hips, round the crotch. Others included *Quan Bu Li Shou, Qu Bu Li Kou* (拳不离手， 曲不离口) which means the fighting ability does not leave the hands, just as music does not leave the mouth. In other words, once you have learned something, you will never forget it. By constant practice, you will not lose an acquired skill. In addition to our regular classes he exhorted me to practise as many hours as I could every day and especially to take advantage of the full-length mirrors in the wushu training hall to observe any faults that might be creeping in and to pay attention to detail. *Ming Cha Qiu Hao* (明察秋毫) - Be sharp-minded enough to perceive the minutest detail and develop an extremely discerning eye.

Guan had a very nice blend of ancient and modern, developing the internal and the external, of making the difficult accessible and of making the simple seem complex. Whereas previously I had struggled with new concepts and movements, he always found the way of opening the gate for me. By first practising the basics before even embarking on the form, I found the movements came more easily. He began like an artist by painting in the background and the broad brushstrokes. He then filled in the detail afterwards. He said there was a *Qiaomen* - a key or a knack to solving any problem or to performing any difficult movement. I had a particular problem with form thirty-six in the Chen routine, Lotus Kick and Drop into the Splits. I could get down into the posture alright but I just couldn't spring back up again into Golden Cock Stands On One Leg. We worked on this for a long time together and I still couldn't perfect it. Guan just seemed to glide up with the minimum of effort whereas I was busting a gut to get my body back off the floor. He never lost patience and even showed me his sense of humour. "Don't worry if you can't do it at first. Can you do this?" He bent his left leg and straightened and extended his right leg resting on the heel. Then he bent forward at the waist and touched the tip of his right foot with his chin. I tried it and couldn't get anywhere near it. "That's impossible," I said. "I'll never be able to do that." "Don't worry," replied Guan. "None of them can do it either." He swept his hand round the training hall to indicate the entire wushu team and their coaches. It was true. Nobody else could do it. It was his little party piece. He smiled, I felt better and I kept on practising. *Shu Neng Sheng Qiao* - Practise makes perfect.

I continued to train three times a week for the next two months until the end of July with Guan Tie Yun. Although he was a very private man and not easy to get to know, we had by this time developed a very strong relationship. I was well integrated into the life of the Institute and was a familiar figure cycling around the campus. Everyone knew *Tuo Ma Si* the crazy English tai chi teacher. I had an especially good friendship with Wen Hui who still attended my classes and cooked my lunch whilst I taught her French. Not only that, Director Zhang of the Foreign Affairs Office commissioned myself and Wen Hui to write a brochure in English to promote the Institute abroad and attract more foreign students. President Li Le Zheng invited me to his house on many occasions where we did a lot of serious research together as well as sharing many jokes as he had a typically English sense of humour. One lunchtime we got drunk in his office. I taught him all the swear words in English and he taught me all the swear words in Chinese until his wife came in and wondered why we were drunk and having so much fun. Life was wonderful. I really enjoyed my weekly routine. I couldn't have asked for any more. I should have known it was too good to last.

For a week or so, Guan Tie Yun hadn't been his usual self. I didn't pay much attention to it at the time. We had finished the Chen style routine and he was helping me to revise the finer details. I was looking forward to learning something different with him. I hadn't decided or discussed it with him yet but I hoped to convince him to teach me the long traditional first form of Chen style. That was my next target. On Saturday the 4th of August, I turned up as usual at 8 o'clock for my three hour lesson. Wen Hui was already there. So was Guan Tie Yun. "I've got some news for you," he said. "I'm leaving." I didn't know what to say. "Leaving," I repeated . "For good?" "No. My friends in Kyoto have invited me to return to Japan to teach them. It's a good opportunity for me." I congratulated him and tried to look as pleased as I could but inside I felt sick. I realised that I had been very lucky to enjoy his undivided attention for the last two months. "Thank you very much for teaching me. It's been an honour and a privilege." I really meant it. He sensed my disappointment and said reassuringly, "Don't worry. I'm coming back." "When?"I asked hopefully. "In eight months. I'll be back next March. Will you still be here?" he asked. "Yes, certainly," I replied. "We can continue then, I hope," he said. "I hope so too," I added. We didn't say much more that lesson. I just wished him *Yi Lu Shun Feng* - Have a good trip. Before he left the training hall, he gave me a copy of a book he had written and in it was the inscription in Chinese "To my student Tuo Ma Si. In the field of wushu friendship, the feeling is deep, the meaning long."

I had come to China to find a master. I didn't really know what I was looking for but assumed that I would know one when I found him. Guan Tie Yun was according to his professional title a sports coach. But to me he was much more than that. He was an expert, a scholar, a champion, a good teacher, someone who commanded respect and much more. Can a coach be a master too? If it were possible, then Guan Tie Yun was indeed a master. Above all else he was a dear friend and I would miss him.

Eight months seemed like a very long time. Eight months before Guan Tie Yun would return. In reality the time passed quite quickly. After the long summer holiday, the new term began at my university on Monday September 3rd and I found myself heavily preoccupied by my new students' classes. Not only that, but I had found an outstanding *Qigong* teacher called Master Yu with whom I studied two or three times a week. Whenever I found something new and exciting I tended to throw myself wholeheartedly into it. I practised my *E Mei Qigong* for an hour and a half every morning during the autumn and winter months until it just got too cold. The winters in Shenyang are brutal with temperatures falling to as low as minus 25, and that's without the wind chill factor. Of course I continued to practise my Chen style but it just wasn't the same without the presence of the guiding hand of my teacher.

A very important and significant event took place in Beijing from the 22nd of September to the 9th of October that year - the Eleventh Asian Games. Perhaps it doesn't carry the same weight as the Olympics, but its arrival had been eagerly awaited in China. The real significance for me lay in its Opening Ceremony. If my enthusiasm for tai chi had been beginning to wane, it was certainly regenerated by what I saw on my television screen that Saturday evening the 22nd of September. Fourteen hundred tai chi players from China and Japan gave a mass performance of the simplified 24 step form. Dressed in their white silk suits, people of all ages and abilities performing tai chi simultaneously was a breathtaking and inspiring sight. It really made me feel that I was a member of one enormous international community which had something in common - the love of tai chi.

For the remaining four months of 1990 my tai chi existence remained quite fulfilled. Two or three times a week I continued to study with Liaoning Senior Coach Liu You Zhen. I was also heavily involved with *Qigong* with Master Yu. And on Saturday mornings I still cycled up to the Sports Institute to practise Chen style with my friend Wu Jia Li who was the head basketball coach and incidentally a tai chi enthusiast. I spent Saturday lunchtime with Wen Hui and frequently visited President Li's house. Life continued in this vein until the Chinese New Year of January 1991 when I returned home briefly to England during the Spring Festival.

At the beginning of March 1991 I telephoned Wen Hui and asked her when Guan Tie Yun was due back from Japan. She told me Saturday the 9th, I asked her to arrange a meeting with Mu Xiu Jie, the head of the wushu department in order to plan the renewal of my training schedule at the Sports Institute. This we did on Monday the 11th at 2 o'clock in the afternoon. Professor Mu was polite but firm. She was well aware that I was looking forward to studying under Coach Guan and was naturally delighted to have such an enthusiastic foreign student. However, for the remainder of the academic year she would choose my teachers for me. I could not study uniquely with Guan Tie Yun. She did not insist but I was well aware that I had no option but to accept her decision. Although at the time I didn't know why, it later became clear to me. Professor Mu had to share my teaching around the other coaches in order to keep them sweet. There was a certain amount of kudos attached to training a foreign student and as in any other walk of life there was professional jealousy and rivalry among sports coaches. Besides, teaching me meant an increase in their monthly salary as I was paying fees for my private tuition. I fully understood and accepted this situation. Anyway, I thought it would be beneficial to compare the standards and teaching methods of other coaches at the Institute.

I gave Mu Xiu Jie a shopping list of things I would like to learn. This included the first long traditional Chen style form, bagua and weapons, especially tai chi sword and sabre. Professor Mu told me she had a pleasant surprise in store for me but couldn't divulge it at that time. My classes were to recommence on Monday the 18th of March from 9:30 till 11:30. I would be learning bagua with a new teacher. I was also given an assurance that I would subsequently be allowed to study Chen style once more with Guan Tie Yun. I was perfectly satisfied with this compromise solution and looked forward to meeting my new teacher the following week.

Imagine my surprise on Monday morning when I arrived at the wushu training hall. The Institute wushu team was just beginning its morning practice under the eye of the men's coach Lu Yong Xiang and the women's coach Zhao Qiu Ju. Professor Mu was also present to keep an eye on the coaches as well as the students. I wondered who was going to keep an eye on me. I began my warm up with some stretching and work on the wall bars and waited for my new teacher to arrive. If it wasn't Guan, Lu or Zhao, it had to be one of the other three whom I didn't know at all well. Finally Mu Xiu Jie came up and said "*Kai shi ba*" - Let's start. My eyes nearly popped out of my head. Professor Mu was going to teach me herself! Mu Xiu Jie had a fearsome reputation. She was extremely strict with both members of staff and her students. She demanded and received the utmost respect. Only the best was good enough. She was an international judge and had officiated at the Asian Games in Beijing the previous year. She was so busy that I couldn't imagine why she had chosen herself to be the first teacher to coach me. I could only surmise that she wanted to assert her authority on the wushu department by being seen to take charge of me. At any rate, as I was a student of Guan Tie Yun and she had a soft spot for him, I only hoped some of the warmth and affection she had for him would rub off on me. Otherwise I was in for a rough ride. At our initial meeting she had told me I was in for a pleasant surprise. Was this it?

I have to admit that the two weeks I spent training with Mu Xiu Jie are a complete blur to me now. We studied a modern bagua competition routine. As with Professor Pang and Coach Liu You Zhen we launched immediately into the form. There was no explanation, no historical or philosophical perspective, no practice of basic techniques and no martial applications. It was purely and simply the form. This approach is not for me to criticise. I chose to train at a Sports Institute where students were coached to reproduce competition routines to an extremely high standard. They were basically young athletes - not intellectuals, not historians, not philosophers and not doctors. Their training was completely geared towards achieving technical excellence. No one could argue with that. The standards achieved were near perfect. But what about the internal content? No mention was ever made of that. I had to play the game by their rules or not at all.

Mu Xiu Jie's approach was that of the archetypal sports coach. She showed me a movement. I copied it. She showed me it again and pointed out my mistakes. I copied it and practised it. And so on to the next movement, section by section to the end of the form. It wouldn't have been so bad if I had been able to rely on her full attention. But she often spotted something she disapproved of on the other side of the wushu training hall and stalked off to deal with it, thus leaving me to fend for myself for long periods. I don't really blame her. The truth is she was just too busy to spend so much time teaching one individual. She had a department to run. So I think we were both relieved when she had finished teaching me the form and could delegate responsibility for my training back to one of her coaches. And who did she choose? Guan Tie Yun. I couldn't have been happier.

Guan had obviously been given strict instruction by Mu Xiu Jie to keep on top of my schedule. I already had a good grounding in Chen style, having previously studied the 56 forms competition routine. This was an amalgamation of the two traditional long forms. In view of my familiarity, we were able to make rapid progress although the traditional movements were subtly different from their modern counterparts. Guan was at pains to point these out to me. Having grooved a particular movement by endless practice, I found it quite difficult at first to override the paths laid down by my muscle memory. It only served to increase the tremendous respect that I had for these sports coaches who retained so many different martial arts disciplines perfectly in their minds. As opposed to our original laid-back classes, these two or three-hour sessions were highly intensive and within the space of two weeks we had completed the first long traditional Chen style form. Professor Mu appeared at our last revision class on Saturday the 6th of April and told me that from the following Monday I would be studying something else. This was the surprise she had been keeping in store for me. Coach Guan would continue to be at my disposal for further revision of the Chen style. But it was time for me to change again.

The coach of the ladies wushu team, Zhao Qui Ju, had been absent for a couple of weeks. I had missed her at squad training which had been taken over entirely by the men's team coach, Lu Yong Xiang. The following training session I discovered where she had been. She had been to the Beijing Wushu Institute for some instruction of her own. Each time a new wushu routine was devised, it had to be disseminated throughout China. This was done by publishing books and demonstration video tapes but primarily by calling all the coaches from the Sports Institutes in the major cities to Beijing in order to receive expert tuition. They would then return to their respective colleges and teach the form to their fellow teachers and their students.

In the field of tai chi, there already existed a combination 42 step championship form containing elements of the four principal styles of tai chi -Yang, Chen, Wu and Sun. However, the only standard tai chi sword form was the 32 step routine which was based on Yang style and was too simple for competition purposes. With the propagation of tai chi as an international sport in mind, it was decided to compile a new and original sword form. Masters representing the four principal styles of tai chi were consulted and together with a committee of tai chi experts and scholars the 42 step tai chi sword form was devised under the guidance of Zhang Shan, Vice-President of the Wushu Research Institute of the Chinese National Sports Commission. Along with the representatives from the other premier Sports Institutes, Zhao Qiu Ju had spent two weeks learning and perfecting the form with Li Bing Ci, one of the masters assigned to pass on the new tai chi championship sword form.

Zhao Qiu Ju was fresh from her trip to Beijing. This was Mu Xiu Jie's pleasant surprise. I was going to study the new sword form with Coach Zhao. I was really excited. Not only was I the first student to learn this sword routine at the Shenyang Sports Institute, but I was probably one of the first foreigners to learn it at all in the whole of China. I got a thrill from studying traditional martial arts but I had to admit that I was equally thrilled to have the privilege of being one of the first to learn a brand new tai chi routine which would eventually establish itself as a championship standard.

To date I had only admired Zhao Qiu Ju from afar. She was a tall, willowy and very attractive lady of about thirty. She always looked smart and gave the impression of elegance and style. She was a graduate of the Shenyang Institute. In her youth she had been the Liaoning Province ladies tai chi champion and in 1984 was the Chinese National Tai Chi sword and double swords champion. She was now the coach of the Institute's ladies' wushu team.

Over the years I have developed a special affection and affinity for the sword - 32 sword, 42 sword, Yang sword, Chen sword and bagua sword. I love them all. Zhao Qiu Ju's nature was perfectly attuned to the sword. She had such a strong yet delicate touch. I was delighted to place myself in her hands. Like Guan Tie Yun, I found Coach Zhao a very patient, sympathetic and methodical teacher with a sense of humour. She had only just learned the form herself so it was fresh in her mind. She began by explaining to me that the form comprised elements which were characteristic of Chen, Yang, Wu and Sun styles. The opening movements and those explosive sword techniques such as *Beng Jian* (Burst With The Sword) and *Tui Jian* (Push The Sword) belonged to Chen style. Movements such as *Ti Xi Pi Jian* (Lift Knee And Chop With The Sword), *Ding Bu Tuo Jian* (Support The Sword In T-Step) and the difficult kicking and simultaneous striking movements such as *Fen Jiao Hou Dian* (Separate The Foot And Point Backwards) and *Hou Ju Tui Jia Jian* (Raise The Leg Backwards And Ward Off With The Sword) all belonged to Wu style. The two consecutive movements at the conclusion of the form *Xing Bu Yun Ci* (Cloud Sword In Walking Step) and *Bai Tui Jia Jian* (Swing Lotus Leg And Ward Off With The Sword) belonged to Sun style. Most of the remaining movements were taken from traditional Yang style. Coach Zhao proceeded to demonstrate to me the various sword techniques. I have to admit that I hadn't been aware that there were so many. Having already learned the 32 step sword form I was aware of techniques such as *Dian* (point), *Ci* (thrust), *Sao* (sweep), *Dai* (carry), *Lan* (parry) and *Pi* (chop). However, she showed me about twenty different sword techniques, almost all of which were present in the form. There didn't seem enough words in the English language to translate them satisfactorily. There were at least three different words in Chinese for to cut which were differentiated by the level and angle of attack. I realised that I had a great deal to learn. Fortunately I was in the hands of a consummate swordswoman.

Everything I learned inside the Sports Institute was modern, competition-orientated wushu. Everything so far with the exception of the traditional long Chen style form which Guan Tie Yun had taught me. I had come to China to find some kind of standardisation and uniformity. The modern specially devised championship routines had given me the consistency I had been searching for. What they lacked, however, was the depth of culture and tradition that an ancient Chinese martial art should possess. I felt that I was learning a lot but understanding very little. I needed more instruction in the traditional arts. The man to teach me was Guan Tie Yun. I approached Coach Guan privately and asked him if he would be willing to teach me outside the Sports Institute. He agreed. I insisted on paying him the twelve yuan an hour that I was paying to the Foreign Affairs Office in order to keep our arrangement on a business footing. I continued to have my classes at the Sports Institute with Zhao Qiu Ju, Mu Xiu Jie and the youngest coach Xu Yi Xun so I didn't feel that I was depriving the Institute of any revenue.

I met Guan Tie Yun at an appointed place in the nearby Beiling Park. The park consisted of enclosed areas of all sizes both large and small where martial arts classes could practise every morning. In a heavily wooded area we found a secluded sandy spot surrounded by overhanging branches which could only be approached by a track through the undergrowth. This was our own secret and private training ground. In the cool early morning air, through the dappled sunlight and on the brushed wet sand, this was an idyllic place. I had asked Guan Tie Yun to teach me traditional bagua. I had already learned a modern competition routine with Professor Mu but was longing to learn a traditional style. Guan Tie Yun had studied bagua under several masters - firstly Sa Guo Zheng from Yunnan Province who was now in his eighties, secondly Xia Bo Hua who was Chief Coach at the Beijing Wushu Research Institute and thirdly Guo Hong Hai from Chengdu, Sichuan Province, who had taught him bagua sword. The style Guan was going to teach me was the "original" form devised by Jiang Rong Qiao. Jiang Rong Qiao was a student of Zhang Zhan Kui who in turn was a disciple of Dong Hai Chuan, regarded as the founder and inventor of bagua.

Thus began one of the most interesting and productive periods of my training in internal arts in China. I had principally come to study tai chi but felt that knowledge of one of the other main internal arts - baguazhang, xingyichuan or liu he ba fa would be complementary to these studies. Besides, I had the opportunity to study with an outstanding teacher. It was equally beneficial and rewarding for Guan as he rarely had the opportunity to pass on these traditional arts and skills to interested students.

I had to admit that the fact that our classes were conducted in secret lent them an extra significance, spice and excitement. I really felt that I was learning something special from a special teacher. Guan Tie Yun would have been just as happy to teach me for nothing. He was bursting with traditional skills and knowledge that none of the modern wushu students were interested in learning. I wondered if the fact that he was so modest and self-effacing actually acted against him. Perhaps he should have been more forthright and self-promoting but it would have been against his character. I asked him about this and he replied with a Chinese maxim. He said, "*Zhu Gao Yu Gong*" (竹高愈躬) - The taller the bamboo, the more it bows. In other words the greater one's achievements, the more modest one should be. That summer I was to find out how true this was in his case. He never told me in advance and he never mentioned this to me afterwards, but I found out from a third party. Guan took part in the Chinese National Traditional Martial Arts Championship for Coaches and Masters. He came first and won gold medals for his performances of yuanyangchuan (Mandarin Duck Boxing) and bagua sword in the weapons category. In his place, I would have felt so proud and been so eager to tell everyone. He said nothing. I respected him all the more for it.

Jiang Rong Qiao's "original" form of bagua is extremely long and complicated. It consists of eight *Zhang* or palms and there are some 179 movements in total. It was an equally daunting task for me as the student and Guan as the teacher. He knew that I was a slow learner but practised hard so he was extremely patient with me. As with the Chen style, Guan spent a long time practising the basic stepping movements and hand position before tackling the form at all. I spent hours and hours just walking the bagua circle in both directions, changing and changing again, taking eight steps each time to complete the circle and with my hands clasped lightly behind my back. I went on to practise basic Single Change Palm and Double Change Palm, gradually introducing the eight hand forms. All the while I was using the characteristic stepping style particular to bagua called *Tang Ni Bu* (蹚泥步) - Mud-wading step. This way of stepping was absent from modern bagua and when I later took part in international competitions in China, I found that I was the only competitor using the traditional way of stepping as if wading through mud and water.

You might imagine that I found this endless practice of basic technique somewhat boring and monotonous. Quite the contrary, I found that simply walking a perfect circle, in eight measured steps, describing that circle on the smooth dew-dropped sand was completely invigorating and fulfilling. It gave me a very deep and mystifying feeling as if I were being hypnotised by the repetitious rhythm. When I eventually added the twisting, diving, spinning and swooping movements, the sense of release from the confines of the circle was quite exquisite. There was a sudden rush of internal power as I initiated Fierce Tiger Leaves the Cage, Hawk Whirls into the Sky or Rhinoceros Looks at the Moon. The names of the movements themselves were heavy with traditional cultural significance. The place where we practised could not have been more appropriate. Many of the names of the movements in bagua belong to the animal kingdom, both real and mythical. There weren't any tigers or hawks but there certainly was animal life in the form of birds, reptiles and insects. Remarkably when I was practising walking the circle by myself - endlessly, slowly, rhythmically walking the circle - the animal life seemed to emerge from the undergrowth, completely oblivious to my presence. It was as if I were invisible. And the butterflies floated and danced around my head as I walked the circle, lightly brushing their powdery wings against my face. Memories of practising bagua in this secluded glade in the summer of 1991 are among my dearest and most cherished.

There are many idioms, maxims and sayings in Chinese. One is *Da Po Sha Guo Wen Dao Di* (打破沙锅问到底) which literally means that you have to break the sand wok in order to get to the bottom. To put it more clearly, if you want to find something out, you just have to keep asking. Another idiom states *Ji Bu Ke Shi, Shi Bu Zai Lai* (机不可失，时不再来) which means an opportunity should not be missed as that opportunity may never come again. In the summer of 1991 I returned to England before flying off to teach in the United States for a while. But true to the idioms, China was inevitably drawing me back once more. I couldn't stay away. It was too big a magnet to resist. Besides I had gone to China to find the answers to some questions. All that I had found was a lot more questions to be answered. What is more, I had been offered a golden opportunity to return. President Li and Director Zhang of the Shenyang Sports Institute offered me a deal. I could become the Institute's resident English teacher, giving twelve hours of lessons a week. In return I would receive twelve hours or more of martial arts instruction. In addition I could live on campus and would receive free accommodation. The only thing I would have to pay for was my meals either in the student dining hall or in the guest house's refectory. As a full time foreign student, I would have had to pay 250 US dollars a month. It was a good deal. I accepted and returned yet again to China. *Bu Ru Hu Xue, Bu De Hu Zi* (不入虎穴，不得虎子) - If you don't go to the tiger's den, you will never get the tiger's cub. I'll leave you to work out the meaning of this idiom for yourself .

"*Ni hai mei zou*?" was a frequent question I was asked around the campus of the Shenyang Institute of Physical Culture by teachers and students alike. It meant "Haven't you gone yet?" or "Are you still here?" I just seemed to keep turning up like a bad penny. In fact I arrived as a full-time teacher and full-time student in the autumn of 1991 and didn't leave for good until June 1993. And even then I didn't actually leave China. I just went to live in the southern Chinese city of Shenzhen where I lived with my wife to be and found myself a genuine Chinese tai chi master. A lot more water had to flow under the bridge until I reached that stage.

My second stint at the Sports Institute was fundamentally different from the first. Before, I was a paying outsider who trained on the fringes of the wushu department, didn't get involved with internal affairs of the college and was seen as something of a novelty. Now I was an insider who lived in college and was a permanent member of staff as well as being a full-time student. I felt more readily accepted and taken more seriously.

I lived in the *Zhao Dai Suo* which was the guest house for visiting experts and students. I could come and go more or less as I pleased although the outside gates of the guest house were locked at 10 p.m. The movements of most foreign teachers in China were fairly restricted. I wasn't sure if it was to save the Chinese people from being inflicted on us or to save us from being inflicted on the Chinese. At any rate the authorities preferred to see us foreigners safely tucked up in our beds by ten o'clock at the latest. I was usually pretty tired by all my training exertions and rose quite early so I didn't view the restriction as much of a hardship.

In the context of the wushu department I was by now definitely an insider. Although at 43 I was more than twice the age of the wushu students, they treated me as one of them. They usually warmed up by playing football with a soft ball in the wushu training hall. The sides were split purely on sexual grounds - the boys against the girls, although I often chose to play for the girls' team just to be perverse. Sometimes I would bamboozle them with my football dribbling skills and bamboozled them even more when I picked up the ball and started to run with it, declaring that we were now playing rugby. They thought I was just a crazy Englishman. They also made fun of the fact that I practised tai chi, being of the opinion that it was only fit for people over sixty. When I did my warm-up and stretching exercises, they imitated me and made accompanying creaking and groaning sounds to simulate my ageing muscles, bones and joints. It was all great fun. In spite of this levity, they still treated me as a serious martial artist. I was always the first to arrive at the wushu training hall in the morning and always the last to leave. I practised religiously. They gave me credit for that. I certainly rose in their estimation when I showed them I could perform the fast external wushu just as well as the slow internal arts. I asked the men's team coach to teach me the competition *Da Dao* (Halberd) form. This was a heavy implement which required a lot of skill and strength. When I'd learned the form and practised it to Coach Lu's satisfaction, I gave the wushu team a demonstration. They nodded approvingly and said, "*Bu cuo*" - Not bad!

On the teaching front I gave some of my lessons in the daytime and some in the evening which allowed me plenty of time for my tai chi classes. Not only did I teach the students but I also taught the sports coaches too. If they wanted to travel abroad, as most of them did, they would have to attain a reasonable level in English. It was my job to coach them to that standard. It was quite a curious sensation to be put in the position of teaching some of my own coaches. I gave them all English names. Guan Tie Yun was Paul because he reminded me of Paul McCartney in looks and nature. Lu Yong Xiang was George not because he reminded me of George Harrison. And Zhao Qiu Ju was Cheryl because ..... well I can't quite remember now. Coach Lu, the trainer of the men's wushu team was a tremendously funny character. In addition to his tracksuit he would always wear a porkpie hat and looked like a seedy second-hand car salesman. George seemed an appropriate name. I also nicknamed him *Da Tui Xiansheng* - Mr Thighs because he had enormously well-developed and shapely thighs. I compared my tai chi sword coach Zhao Qiu Ju to Lady Diana which flattered her and made her blush. We had a lot of fun in our English lessons and they learned more quickly as a result of it. I had a high-energy style of teaching which they seemed to appreciate and I was often more shattered after one of my English lessons than after one of my three hour tai chi training sessions.

Until the end of the summer term 1992, I continued to add more to my internal martial arts repertoire. I learned traditional Yang style sabre under Mu Xiu Jie. I studied pushing hands and bagua sword with Guan Tie Yun. And of course I learned halberd with George. More than anything, I used this time to consolidate and practise what I had learned. There was the temptation to go on learning, adding even more forms to my repertoire. However, I realised that it was more important to practise what I already had and so set about revising, honing and perfecting with the aid of my teachers.

During this period I was fortunate enough to attend several national competitions. In early May I travelled with the Shenyang team to Nanchang, the capital of Jiangxi Province, to take part in the Chinese National Wushu Team Championships. Then in July I went to the city of Jinzhou in Liaoning Province for the Chinese National Tai Chi and Pushing Hands Championships. Later that month I supported the Shenyang team once more at the Chinese National Sports Institutes Championships in Tianjin. Generally speaking I was the only foreigner at these events and I have kept details of these competitions for the second book to be published in this series.

In the August of 1992 I graduated in internal martial arts from the Shenyang Institute of Physical Culture and received my graduation certificate and medal. I felt so proud and yet so sad that it had come to an end. Actually it hadn't come to an end at all. Far from it. In October I was back in Shenyang for another eight months with another purpose in mind. In view of my linguistic skills and my interest in Chinese martial arts as well as western sports, I had been commissioned along with President

Li Le Zheng to write an English language handbook for Olympic sports coaches by the Chinese National Sports Commission. It comprised more than thirty sports and ran to a third of a million words. It kept me occupied night and day for more than six months. I also had my own English language radio programme broadcast throughout the North of China. I appeared on TV chat shows. And I renewed acquaintance with the young Chinese lady who was to become my wife. Please do not think that I have skimmed so lightly over these and other important events. They too will form part of the subject matter of the third book in this series. It is difficult not write about them now but I must bite my tongue and bring this chapter to a close.

All told, my association with the Shenyang Institute of Physical Culture lasted from May 1990 until May 1993. I can honestly say that this was one of the happiest periods of my existence. It regenerated my whole outlook on life, turned it around and made me a better person with a real and positive purpose. After suffering the build-up to, the agony of and the aftermath to Tian An Men Square, my faith in China and my faith in myself had been shaken. There is a saying in Chinese : *Ye Luo Gui Gen* (叶落归根) which means literally that when a leaf falls, it will return to its root. It was usually applied to Chinese people living abroad. An overseas Chinese will always be drawn back to his original ancestral roots. As a foreigner I felt my cultural roots lay in China. That's why I kept on going back time after time. Of course my declared purpose was to seek and find the roots of tai chi. Equally I was looking for my own roots. In the Shenyang Institute I found outstanding teachers, lifelong friendships and mutual respect. The study and practice of tai chi is inextricably bound up with the development of one's moral character. *Jing Ren Zhe, Ren Heng Jing Zhi* (敬人者， 人恒敬之) - Someone who respects others is always respected by others. At the Shenyang Institute I learned humility in the presence of the modesty of such great teachers as Guan Tie Yun and I earned the respect of everyone for my diligence, perseverance and sincerity and above all my love of China.

Great Grandmaster Fu Zhong Wen explains the finer points of Tai Chi.

Guan Tie Yun with the author in the Wushu training hall.

Li Xiao Ling with the author performing Chen style movement called Sword Facing the Morning Sun.

Zhao Qiu Ju showing movement called Lean with Body in Horse Riding Step.

Author doing Chen style movement Tuck in Robes.

Chen style: Cover Hands and Strike with Arm.

Bat Falls to the Earth: a movement from Jiang Rong Qiao's form of Baguazhang (Pa Kua Chang).

Jinzhou Railway Athletic Sports Hall: venue for the 1992 Chinese National Tai Chi and Pushing Hands Championships.

Chinese National Olympic Stadium: venue for the Beijing International Wushu and Taijiquan Invitational Tournament.

Yin-Yang symbol referred to in following chapter

YI JIAN SHUANG DIAO

（一箭双雕）

ONE ARROW TWO TARGETS

Shenyang is the capital city of Liaoning Province. It is the fourth largest city in China and is one of its most important industrial centres, lying as it does at the heart of the communication and transportation network of the north-eastern region. Its prosperity is built on coal mining, iron and steel, heavy engineering, textiles and chemicals. The city's climate is brutal in the extreme, from hot, dry, windy and dusty in the summer to heavy snows and temperatures touching minus 25 in the winter.

Shenzhen is a special economic zone which lies just across the border from Hong Kong in Guangdong Province. In the 1970's it was a small fishing village but because of its strategic location, it was targeted for rapid development. It is now one of the richest and fastest-growing cities in China. It is the hi-tech capital of the country with a proliferation of telecommunications and computer businesses, attracting joint ventures and foreign investment from all over the world. Its climate is humid and sub-tropical and it suffers from torrential rains and typhoons.

How on earth did I find myself transported from Shenyang to Shenzhen in the spring of 1993? The answer quite simply is a woman. As a result of appearing on the TV chat show "*Hai Wai Feng Qing*", I was reunited with one of my fellow teachers and postgraduate English students from the Shenyang Pharmaceutical University called Lu Shuo. The relationship developed and we began going out together. It wasn't easy. In the conservative, traditional city of Shenyang it was frowned upon for Chinese women to associate with foreigners. People took the view "Why isn't a Chinese man good enough for you ?" It was impossible for us to carry on our relationship in public and we nearly got into some serious trouble on one occasion, almost getting ourselves arrested. Lu Shuo was a very clever, ambitious woman and wanted to further her career. She had a degree in computer science. The logical step seemed to be to try her hand in the special economic zone of Shenzhen which was crying out for young people with her talent and qualifications. In April 1993 she packed up, left home and went to seek a new life, a new home and a new job in Shenzhen. It was a very courageous step for a young woman to take. Meanwhile I returned home briefly to England the same month before going back to Shenyang on the 7th of May. I confided my secret in President Li Le Zheng and asked if he had any contacts in Shenzhen. Two former students from the Shenyang Sports Institute, Wang Xin and An Xu, were now resident in Shenzhen. President Li phoned them and asked them to assist me on my arrival in Shenzhen. It was as simple as that. I had no idea where I was going to live. I had no idea what I was going to do for a living. I was simply driven by the desire to be with the woman I loved. Or was it fate once again playing its part?

I took the 9:20 a.m. flight from Shenyang on Monday the 31st of May and arrived in Shenzhen at 12:55. The temperature was 30 degrees and there was 87% humidity. I got a bus into town and was met at the station by my new friends from Shenyang. It was like home from home. But Shenzhen could not have been more different from Shenyang. Shenyang was a massive urban sprawl, dark with heavy industry and pollution. Shenzhen was a bright , new vibrant city with skyscrapers. It looked like Dallas. It was hard to believe this was China. There seemed to be more Mercedes and BMWs than bicycles and there was a McDonald's on every corner. This wasn't the China that I knew, but it was still China and all the more exciting for it. My friends had booked me into a room at the guesthouse of the Technical College in the north of the city. The following morning they picked me up in a car and took me to the Foreign Languages Institute. They already had a Canadian foreign teacher. He suggested I should try the Education and Careers Training Centre. They might have some teaching work but only in the evening. Back at the Technical College I went to the English department to enquire if they needed a native English teacher. They didn't but they suggested that I should try next door at the Shenzhen College of Education. As a new city there were relatively few colleges, institutes and universities unlike in Shenyang. There was a university but it was situated on a campus some forty minutes by bus from the centre of town. I decided to try my hand next door. The College of Education was a brand new building on the city's ringroad just opposite the International Exhibition Centre. It was a teacher training college and TOEFL (Test of English as a Foreign Language) centre. I was directed to the English department on the fourth floor where I was fortunate enough to bump into the head of the department, Professor Xie and one of his colleagues Mrs Lin. He was very interested. Their English teacher had just left and they were desperately looking for a replacement. He took me immediately to see the College President. I could teach for ten hours a week, would have a rent-free three-room flat in the Chinese teachers building and would receive a monthly salary of 1200 yuan, half of it being exchanged into US dollars. Once again my luck had held out. I had landed on my feet. I moved in the following Monday morning.

It was actually near the end of the summer term and the new autumn term wouldn't start until the 1st of September. I taught three weeks of classes until the end of June which gave me some time to get to know my students. Having told them of my interest in tai chi, they suggested that I should go to Lizhi Park in the centre of town to seek out some likeminded people with whom I could study or practise. I took up their suggestions and let myself in for a very pleasant surprise.

By the time I arrived in Shenzhen I had given up all hope of finding a real Chinese tai chi master. Of course I hadn't actually looked very hard. I had rather been led by my destiny. Besides, in the coaches at the Shenyang Institute of Physical Culture such as Guan Tie Yun, Zhao Qiu Ju and Mu Xiu Jie, I felt that I had been instructed to the highest possible level. As a foreign tai chi teacher, I reckoned that my standards were already superfluously high for the kinds of people who wanted to learn back home in England. At this stage I was really doing it for myself, my self-satisfaction and my self-fulfilment. As far as I was concerned, my tai chi education had practically reached its end. All that was left for me to do was to practise. I had principally come to Shenzhen to support my Chinese girlfriend in her professional ambitions, to live in a more open, relaxed environment where our relationship could grow unhindered and without prejudice, to experience a different part of China and to continue to live in a country whose culture I loved.

The newly developed special economic zone of Shenzhen was the last place that I would have expected to find the traditional roots of tai chi. You would be hard pressed to find anywhere in China less steeped in tradition than this ultramodern city. I didn't expect the standard of teachers in the park to be too high either. I imagined that having newly graduated from the Shenyang Institute, my standard would be much higher than theirs. I couldn't have been more wrong. On Sunday the 20th of June, I made my way to Li Zhi Park in downtown Shenzhen at about seven o'clock in the morning. What I saw at first confirmed my expectations. I witnessed groups practising the 42 tai chi chuan and tai chi sword forms. I saw some simplified 24 step tai chi and some competition Chen style. In addition there was some bagua and several qigong classes.

Most of the teachers had embroidered banners hanging from the lower branches of the trees to advertise their classes. My eye was caught by one class whose publicity material was a string of old photographs, magazines and newspaper cuttings. I couldn't quite see the teacher as he was fairly small and was surrounded by a large group of people who seemed to be hanging on his every word. I examined the photographs carefully and saw the picture of someone I recognised. It was Great Grandmaster Fu Zhong Wen, doyen of traditional Yang family style tai chi and leading disciple of Yang Cheng Fu. I had read articles and seen photographs of him in "China Sports" and "Martial Arts of China".

One of the group spotted me and told their teacher. In an instant the group had surrounded me and as a gap opened up I saw striding towards me a short, muscular man of about sixty wearing a transparently thin white silk tai chi suit. He shook my hand and, apart from being very strong, I could feel that his palm was extremely warm. He introduced himself as Mei Ying Sheng and proceeded to introduce his wife and daughter who also assisted him in the class. His daughter, Ao Shuang, also spoke extremely good English, as did his principal student Chi Hui. Mei seemed surprised that I knew who Fu Zhong Wen was. He asked me if I was interested in tai chi. When I replied that not only was I interested, but that I was actually a tai chi teacher from England who had already been studying in China for four years, he was even more surprised. I could see that Mei Ying Sheng appeared in the photographs with Fu Zhong Wen and that he was the author of the magazine articles on display- "*Fu laoshi shi wo de laoshi*" (Master Fu is my teacher) he said. It just so happened that I had learned the thirteen forms Yang style tai chi sabre routine at the Shenyang Institute from Professor Mu Xiu Jie. She had incidentally learned it from Fu Zhong Wen in Shanghai. Mei Ying Sheng was absolutely delighted to hear this. I told him that I had practised the long 108 step traditional Yang style form in England for nearly ten years but wasn't entirely satisfied with its authenticity. Since I had been in China I had learned the 40 forms Yang style competition routine with Liu You Zhen, Senior Coach of the Liaoning Province Wushu Team.

Mei insisted that I should give him and the class a demonstration of the modern Yang style form and the traditional sabre form. The class cleared an area and sat down to watch as I launched into my display. With the benefit of hindsight, on previous occasions that I had given demonstrations I realised that my standard had been quite poor. However, at this stage in my tai chi education, I knew that my tai chi was pretty good even by Chinese standards. I was confident but not over-confident. When I had finished, the group applauded politely but this time I think it was because they were genuinely impressed. Mei Ying Sheng rose and asked me to watch. He told me that he himself had devised a short traditional Yang style routine consisting of 36 movements which had been approved by the governing body of Yang style tai chi in China. He was going to perform this for me followed by another Yang style sabre routine consisting of 40 movements which had been devised by Li Chun Nian, one of the earliest disciples of Yang Cheng Fu. I sat down in the shade to watch.

When I first arrived in China, I had been impressed by anyone with a Chinese face practising martial arts. This phenomenon is widespread in the West where Chinese teachers are considered superior simply because of the way that they look. After several years in China I certainly didn't suffer from this affliction any longer and I wasn't easily impressed. I had been to the Chinese National Tai Chi Championship and had seen national champions such as Chen Si Tan and Gao Jia Min. In fact I have to say that I had become rather blasé. My familiarity with excellence made me very hard to impress indeed.

However, having seen Mei Ying Sheng, I have to admit to revising the criteria by which I judged the standards of excellence in tai chi. It was on an altogether different plane. The first thing that struck me was that although this was a physical demonstration, Mei Ying Sheng made it feel like an out of body experience. It was as if his body had been turned inside out and we were watching the internal rather than the external being. It was quite remarkable. Every movement flowed quite naturally and beautifully into the next. It was soft and aesthetically pleasing whilst at the same time being robust, hard and martial. My dilemma in trying to reconcile tai chi as a sport, a martial art, a form of meditation, a health promoting art and a traditional art was at an end. All these contradictory yet complementing functions were synthesised in Mei's performance. The opening and closing of the postures, the transition from Yin to Yang and from Yang to Yin were so clearly demonstrated in his form. His performance said more than words could express. I was completely overcome with awe and admiration. I knew that, at long last without actually looking, I had found a real tai chi Master.

The question was what was he doing here in Shenzhen of all places? The class broke up at 9 and about a dozen of us retired to the restaurant on the edge of the park to take *Zao Cha* - morning tea, a traditional late breakfast in Canton Province consisting mainly of *dim sums* with large pots of chrysanthemum tea drunk with sugar. I had noticed that his main student Chi Hui who worked for the Shenzhen Daily Newspaper addressed him as Doctor Mei. This was explained by the fact that Mei Ying Sheng was a retired medical practitioner and acupuncturist. He came originally from Le Shan in Sichuan Province in the far west of China. It was close to Mount Emei, one of the four famous Buddhist mountains in China and famous for its colossal twelfth century Sitting Buddha cut out of the rock face. From one of China's sacred cultural centres, Dr Mei moved with his wife and younger daughter to Shenzhen for a complete change of scene and to give Ao Shuang the opportunity to follow her career. She too, like my girlfriend Lu Shuo, wanted to pursue her profession in the hi-tech capital of China. I couldn't believe my luck. In Sichuan Province Doctor Mei had studied with fifth generation Yang style masters who were disciples of Li Chun Nian from Chengdu. Then in the 1980's he had gone to Shanghai to study with fourth generation Grandmaster Fu Zhong Wen. In 1983 he was awarded the title of outstanding martial arts instructor by the Chinese National Wushu Association. In addition, he was a member of the Council of the China Yongnian International Tai Chi Chuan Association, the governing body for traditional Yang style tai chi in China.

Doctor Mei loved to talk about tai chi. He was very curious about the extent to which tai chi was practised in Europe and North America and exhorted me to do my best to popularise it and propagate it as much as I could once I returned to England. I hadn't anticipated learning any more tai chi at that moment in time. I had been quite happy practising my competition forms, my sword and sabre and my bagua. Having seen Doctor Mei, I was forced to reconsider my position. As we parted, he invited me to return to the park for the evening class. He would be delighted to share my knowledge and if I liked, I could join his next class. I thanked him for his invitation and said that I would think it over. But inside I knew that I had already made up my mind.

Master Mei's classes worked in rotation. He taught the short 36 step routine, followed by the long sword form, and finally the long traditional 85 step tai chi form as devised by Yang Cheng Fu. Interspersed with these classes were sessions dedicated to pushing hands and occasional intensive weekend classes in tai chi sabre. By a stroke of luck he was just at the beginning of a new cycle and on the following Saturday, the 26th of June he would begin teaching the short tai chi form. It was a temptation I could not resist. During the week between our first meeting and the beginning of a new class, I did a lot of hard, deep thinking. On the one hand, I felt that I already knew enough tai chi. In fact I had already stopped practising some routines as I felt that I had learned too much and needed to pare my repertoire to its barest minimum. On the other hand, fate had dealt me this opportunity. If I didn't seize it, I knew that I would live to regret it. That morning's demonstration had dealt a blow to my self-confidence. I had become quietly smug and filled with self-satisfaction at the level of tai chi I had attained. My ego had been well and truly deflated. There is a Chinese idiom *Ren Wai You Ren, Tian Wai You Tian* (人外有人， 天外有天) which means literally that apart from this person (you), there is another person; apart from this sky, there is another sky. In other words, there is always someone better than yourself. There is always something better to strive for. Almost at the point when I had stopped searching, when I was preparing to admit that I had reached the maximum of my potential, another door had opened and an opportunity to reach an even higher sky presented itself to me. There is another saying which seemed appropriate to my state of mind at that time : *Qian Shou Yi, Man Zhao Sun* (谦受益， 满招损) which means modesty can be beneficial, whereas self-satisfaction can be harmful. I rediscovered the modesty that I had so admired in Guan Tie Yun and rekindled my desire to be never satisfied with my achievements. I found that Chinese idioms, maxims and sayings played an increasely prominent part in my Chinese existence. As my language skills improved , so did my understanding of the culture. The language of tai chi is rich in its traditional and cultural heritage.

San Ju Hua Bu Li Ben Hang (三句话不离本行) is an idiom that would sum up Master Mei. It means that in any three sentences, a person cannot help talking about something he is interested in. I found that Master Mei only ever talked about tai chi and nothing else. He ate, drank and slept tai chi. He lived in his white silk tai chi suit as if it were a second skin. His whole life was dedicated to the art of tai chi. And by tai chi he meant specifically traditional Yang family style tai chi. In his past he had practised other kinds such as simplified tai chi, the standard 48 form, the 88 forms and so on. But when he had discovered Yang style as taught to him by traditional masters such as Fu Zhong Wen and Gu Liu Xin, he had discarded all the rest. He was now dedicated solely and obsessively to Yang style and regarded it as a jewel in the Chinese national cultural heritage. His enthusiasm was infectious. It was difficult not to be affected by him.

His routine varied little from one day to the next. He rose at six, did some qigong exercises and arrived at Li Zhi Park to begin the class at seven. At eight, half the class would leave to go to work. The rest, including myself and those who had retired, would continue for another hour. After this he would return for breakfast and further discussion if any people were available. Following an early lunch he would sleep for a couple of hours before reading, studying, writing and doing research into tai chi for the remainder of the afternoon. He studied the Tai Chi Classics, the words and photographs of his teachers and other famous masters, seeking to analyse, refine and perfect the art of tai chi. He was a genuine scholar. From a background in medicine and acupuncture it was hardly surprising that amongst the many articles and learned treatises that he wrote, many took as their theme the health related aspects of tai chi, as a form of preventive or curative medicine. In the evening Master Mei returned to Li Zhi Park for another two hour tai chi group session from 7:30 to 9:30. This was quite a strenuous regime for a man of sixty but he thrived on it. If our classes had to be cancelled or suspended due to the torrential monsoon rains and typhoons that frequently struck Shenzhen, he simply did not know what to do with himself. This single-minded dedication was a shining example to us all.

Having attained an advanced level of tai chi even by Chinese standards, I returned to novice status and put myself in the hands of Master Mei. At seven o'clock on the morning of the 26th of June I lined up in the beginners' class. Mei Ying Sheng loved to talk. For the first half an hour we sat around on the grass whilst he talked about the history, philosophy and significance of traditional Yang style. We never did anything before it had been completely explained to us in the minutest detail beforehand. Eventually we lined up facing south. Mei explained to us that when beginning the practice of tai chi you should be facing in a north-south direction to bring your body into alignment with the earth's north/south magnetic field. Strictly speaking men should face south and women north but for the purpose of the class, everyone was to face south. This was in theory to bring the north star in opposition to the point at the base of the skull known in acupuncture as the *Naohu*. In the past my teachers had left me full of unanswered questions. Master Mei seemed to answer questions before I posed them and even answered questions that I hadn't even thought of yet.

Mei Ying Sheng often referred to the Tai Chi Classics and the Ten Essential Points for the correct practice of tai chi as laid down by Yang Cheng Fu. In the ready position with the feet together and the arms hanging loosely by the side with the armpits open and the palms of the hands facing inwards, we should concentrate on *Han Xiong Ba Bei* (含胸拔背) - holding the chest inwards so allowing the breath/*Qi* to sink to the *Dan Tian* and lifting or rounding the back whilst at the same time loosening and relaxing the waist - *Song Yao* (松腰). Paying attention to these requirements should enable you to be both rooted and flexible. Having opened the stance and begun to raise the arms up to shoulder height with the hands palm down, we should focus on *Chen Jian Zhui Zhou* (沉肩坠肘) - sink the shoulders and keep the elbows down and lowered. If the shoulders were raised, the Qi would unwantedly rise to the chest and the application of energy would be misdirected. Mei stressed the isolation of every joint moving and connecting with the next joint, eventually pulling down through the hips, legs, feet and into the ground, whilst at the same time pulling up from the waist and lifting your back. The combination of all these movements enabled you to be firmly rooted in each and every posture and to achieve equilibrium. The class continued to practise the opening stance and commencing form until Master Mei was satisfied that everyone understood the concepts fully and had achieved a physical sensation of these essential requirements.

Every member of the Mei family was involved in the class. He himself talked and demonstrated. Sometimes to save himself or when a particularly demanding technique was required, he would call on the assistance of his daughter, Mei Ao Shuang. In fact Master Mei would often say to me "Don't watch me. Watch my daughter." He explained that this was because he couldn't see himself and therefore couldn't correct himself, but he could see her. Every teacher knows that without the guidance of his own teacher, slight deviations from standard may creep into the form. In addition, as he got older he was not able to perform certain techniques as well as in his younger days. I have observed many instances of students taught by ageing coaches and masters who have duplicated and copied their teachers' movements precisely, not realising that these were the movements of old men and not the same as they would have practised them at the age of 30, 40 or 50. Mei did not fall into this trap. Mei Ying Sheng's wife also assisted in the proceeding. She made her way around the class correcting students' postures. But her most important role was in another area. As her husband used quotations, maxims and idioms, she would write them in chalk on the path in Chinese characters to form a written record of the class. At the conclusion I would always write everything down and go through the explanation of each one with Master Mei.

The most important visual aid that Mei Ying Sheng used was the outline of the *Tai Chi Tu* (the tai chi diagram) of the two entwined black and white fishes on a large piece of cloth which he spread out on the grass in front the class for all to see. No other teacher in my experience had made reference to the diagram so extensively and certainly not with regard to the individual movements and postures of the form. According to Master Mei, the tai chi diagram was a Daoist symbol depicting the two opposing yet complementary forces of Yin and Yang which maintained harmony and equilibrium in the universe. The diagram was made up of two fishes, one black and one white. Each fish was composed of five parts - the head, eye, back, stomach and tail. Every movement in tai chi was either Yin or Yang. In addition, many movements actually mirrored the shape of the tai chi diagram. From the ready position, the arms were raised from the fish's tail up the fish's back until the hands were palms down at shoulder height. By bending the arms and sinking the elbows, the hands came over the top of the fish's head before pushing down and away slightly into the fish's stomach, then finally returning to the hips as they reached the fish's tail once more. This was only one of many examples. Certain fixed postures depicted the centre line of the tai chi diagram. Two that sprung to mind were White Crane Spreads Its Wings and Strike the Tiger. In such a way, Master Mei was able to show us that the movements and postures of the Yang style form could be seen as a reflection of the tai chi diagram.

Mei Ying Sheng turned the usual learning process inside out. He began with the internal which led to the external. This was the reverse of the process that I was used to with my previous teachers, for whom the form was paramount. That is not to say that Master Mei neglected the external. He could not have been more precise. He did, however, make it clear that the outer form was a reflection of the inner content. According to the Tai Chi Classics, the internal energy drives the outer form and the outer form guides the internal energy. The two had a mutually active and complementary effect on each other. Master Mei was of the opinion that the way most people practised tai chi was too easy. There was very little superficial external movement particularly from the waist and consequently very little corresponding internal content. Movements especially around the abdomen and waist were instrumental in generating *Chan Si Jin*, the reeling-silk energy more commonly associated with Chen style tai chi but which also formed an integral part of the correct practice of Yang style tai chi. This twisting and spiralling motion helped to naturally massage the internal organs and the cardiovascular system. Master Mei likened this process to twisting a wet cloth from which the water was effectively wrung. So on the one hand the movements should be soft on the outside, whilst on the other hand the movements should be vigorous on the inside.

That first day and every subsequent day I returned for the evening class from 7:30 to 9:30 in Li Zhi Park. This later session took the form of revision of what had already been covered that morning plus some additional information and refinements. It also gave us the opportunity to practise under his eagle eye. Our evening training pitch was under a light in one corner of the park but quite often the light was broken and we regularly trained in semi-darkness. I found this a help rather than a hindrance. My balance had always been pretty good but I found that practising in the dark was extremely helpful in improving my balance even more and rooting my stances. When the light was working, quite large groups of casual onlookers usually gathered and we often picked up new students as a result. Master Mei did pay special attention to me because I was a foreigner and because he instilled into me my role of promoting traditional Yang style tai chi on my eventual return to the West. Of course, it was an added attraction for him to have a foreign student in his class but he never took advantage of me or abused me as certain teachers had done in the past. I felt proud to have him as a teacher and I think he felt proud to have me as a student . It was a case of mutual respect. Although I was special, it was important for me to feel part of a group. Some people came morning and evening. Others attended either the morning or the evening session. I attended both so my circle of acquaintances grew quite rapidly out of my practice of tai chi. Tai chi is a means of communicating in itself and its shared activity gives people something very special in common. Apart from this social context, this was actually the first time that I had practised as part of a group. Previously I had been one to one with my teachers which is also rewarding in itself. Group performance is particularly beneficial in stimulating and increasing the generation of *Qi*. It may enhance the strength and quality of *Qi* within each individual as well as developing a field or pool of *Qi* around the whole group. Personal development through tai chi is equally as important as the group ethos.

As a medical practitioner Mei Ying Sheng stressed the health aspects and benefits of practising traditional tai chi. At the Shenyang Sports Institute, I had studied acupuncture as a separate subject with Professor Piao, but my coaches had never mentioned it in the direct context of tai chi. Master Mei stressed that the expression of the whole form was in the hands and the hand formation particular to Yang style was called Lotus Leaf Palm. This was formed by naturally spreading and extending the fingers and thumb. The centre of the palm should be slightly concave with the fingers slightly bent. The hand would thus resemble a lotus leaf floating on the water. The correct formation of Lotus Leaf Palm served to open the channels or meridians of the body and to regulate the circulation of *Qi* energy. Of the twelve main meridians in the body, six had their terminal points in the hands. Therefore, during the practice of tai chi, the circulation of *Qi* was best expressed and felt in the hands. Not only that, but there was a difference in the shape of the hand depending on whether one was in a *Yin* posture or a *Yang* posture. In a *Yin* posture, the hand should be soft and relaxed with the palm hollowed, the fingers bent and reasonably close together. Mei Ying Sheng called this *Yin Zhang* (Yin palm). In a *Yang* posture, the hand should be expanded, the fingers separated and extended with the thumb and index finger forming the shape of a tiger's mouth. This was *Yang Zhang* (Yang palm). During this process, the hand would become warm, red and swollen. This was the same extremely warm tingling sensation that I had felt when I first shook hands with Mei Ying Sheng. In my previous tai chi practice with teachers and coaches, this had never been mentioned to me. The hand was just loose and relaxed throughout, to the extent that it was almost lifeless. The constant changing from *Yin* palm to *Yang* palm made a great deal of sense and allowed the *Qi* energy to flow smoothly along the channels and meridians. If anyone ever doubted the existence of these meridians, one only had to closely examine the palms of Mei Ying Sheng on which the lines were clearly discernible. Not only was Master Mei able to explain these phenomena, he could provide living proof of their existence.

Mei Ying Sheng stressed the importance of having a passing knowledge of traditional Chinese medicine and especially the body's network of meridians and acupuncture points. The traditional storehouse of energy in the body was said to be the *Dan Tian*. This was most widely understood to be the point just below the navel known in acupuncture as the *Qi Hai*. In fact this was the lower *Dan Tian*. In all there were three *Dan Tians* lying on the *Ren* Meridian at the front of the body. The middle *Dan Tian* known as the *Shan Zhong* was situated at the intersection of the centre line of the body and the line between the two nipples. The upper *Dan Tian*, known as the *Yin Tang*, was found at the centre point between the eyebrows. One of the twelve main meridians was the Pericardium Meridian of the Hand (*Jue Yin*). It ran from the sack surrounding the heart through the chest at the point known as the *Dian Chi* down the inside of the arm, through the point at the centre of the palm called the *Lao Gong* to the tip of the middle finger, the *Zhong Chong*. The *Lao Gong* point was particularly important. On the inside of the palm it was called the *Nei Lao Gong* and the corresponding point on the back of the hand was the *Wai Lao Gong*. Both points were considered especially strong in transmitting or receiving *Qi* energy. The three *Dan Tians* could store *Qi* and aid in the circulation of *Qi* within the body. They could also produce an outward emission of energy. This was also true of the *Lao Gong* which was used as an instrument of healing by doctors in traditional Chinese medicine as I had witnessed on my first visit to Shenyang when observing Doctor Liu treating patients with *Qigong*. When the hands crossed, palm to palm or back to back or when the *Lao Gong* of either palm passed directly in front of any of the *Dan Tians*, a transmission, exchange or collection of *Qi* could take place. Master Mei told us that this collection of energy was known as *Long Qi* and could be experienced in the hands as a sensation of heat, numbness or swelling. There were many movements within the Yang style form that produced a sensation of internal energy brought about by the correct alignment of critical acupuncture points. They were instrumental in opening up the meridians, regulating the circulation of *Qi* energy and balancing *Yin* and *Yang*.

After the first month of studying with Mei Ying Sheng I had to completely rethink my outlook on tai chi. I had previously studied it as an external sports event whilst simultaneously studying and practising *E Mei Qigong* and acupuncture with other teachers. The problem was that I had never actually drawn them all together. It was my fault for approaching these compatible and overlapping disciplines in a blinkered manner. Perhaps it was the lack of consistency in approach that was at fault and the fact that I had not been systematic and methodical in my learning process of tai chi. Basically I had taken what I had found or what I had been offered. I had been guilty of *San Ri Da Yu, Liang Ri Shai Wang* (三日打鱼， 两日晒网) - Every three days going fishing and every two days putting the nets out in the sun. Of course that was before I met Mei Ying Sheng who was the embodiment of expertise in tai chi, *Qigong* and acupuncture. I could go fishing with him every day and never need to dry my nets in the sun.

My immediate reaction on completion of learning the short traditional Yang form was to stop practising all the other forms of tai chi that I had learned at the Shenyang Sports Institute. I only practised the traditional bagua and bagua sword as taught to me by Guan Tie Yun. Master Mei himself only ever practised traditional Yang style. If it was good enough for him, surely it was good enough for me. Naturally in the course of his own tai chi education spanning some forty odd years he had begun with the simplified 24 forms routine and worked his way up to his present status. I had cast my net widely to find out what I would haul in. My catch in tai chi terms had been wide and various both in terms of my teachers and what they had taught me. On reflection it was too early in my tai chi journey to start discarding indiscriminately. After a lay-off of several weeks, I started to practise the tai chi competition forms once more. I had moved onto another stage of my tai chi education with Mei Ying Sheng but I was still bound by my sense of the duty and respect that I owed to my previous teachers.

The summer holidays came to an end and term restarted at the Shenzhen College of Education on the 1st of September. By this time I was quite accustomed to my new life in a new city. The subtropical climate affected my lifestyle. Every weekend there seemed to be a fresh typhoon and my flat was flooded even though I was on the first floor. I lost a lot of weight partly because of my rigorous tai chi training and partly because there was no air-conditioning in my apartment and the climate was so humid. I lived in a permanent pool of sweat. My bedroom and living room were infested with rats and giant flying cockroaches and there were ants in my kitchen. Not to mention the mosquitoes who managed to penetrate my mosquito net and sting me to death every night. It was quite an existence. I was kept sane by my girlfriend and my tai chi. And by a welcome visitor. On Monday the 19th of September I went to the Airport to pick up President Li Le Zheng who had come to join me for a week. He had brought with him the final proofs of the book that we had been instructed to write together for the Chinese National Sports Commission called "*Tiyu Jiaolianyuan Yingyu*" (体育教练员英语) - English for Sports Coaches. It was wonderful to spend a week with my dearest friend from Shenyang. We shared a lot of fond memories and I caught up on the latest news of the Sports Institute. We spent most of the time pouring over our manuscript. I had personally invested six months of my life virtually 24 hours a day into the writing of this book and I was dying to see it in print. I would have to wait for the summer of the following year for that satisfaction. It was a happy week spent with President Li but tinged with sadness. On the 23rd of September we watched television as the winner of the Olympic bid for the year 2000 was announced. Beijing led the field on the first three ballots and for one glorious moment when time stood still it looked as though we had won it. But our elation and celebration were short-lived. It was a mistake. Sydney had just edged Beijing out of top spot on the fourth ballot. Neither myself nor President Li could help shedding a tear. Hopes had been so high. China was definitely going to be the country of the new century and the new millennium. Everyone's hopes were so high. But it was not to be. And we would have to wait a little longer for wushu and tai chi in particular to be acknowledged as an Olympic event. I still dreamed of that day.

Mei Ying Sheng described the sword as the prince of weapons. Having already learned the 32 sword, 42 sword and bagua sword forms, I was dying to learn traditional Yang style sword. It was my favourite weapon and this Yang style routine became my favourite sword form. Although broadsword or sabre was more spectacular than the sword, being practised at a faster speed and with many circling, winding, chopping and hacking techniques, I preferred the more delicate and subtle touch of the sword. Besides, the broadsword only had one striking edge whereas the sword was a double-edged weapon. Another major difference was in the role of the empty hand. With tai chi broadsword, the empty hand was in the shape of a palm and acted principally as a counterbalance to the hand wielding the sabre. With tai chi sword, the free hand was closed into swordfingers with the middle and index fingers extended and the ring and little fingers bent in towards the palm whilst being pressed down with the thumb. Swordfingers served the purpose of balancing up the energy in the body with the sword as well as being used to attack your opponent's vulnerable points. The sword itself should be viewed merely as an extension of the hand and arm with the qi energy being directed to the tip or to a particular part of the cutting edge.

I had studied the 42 tai chi competition sword form with Coach Zhao Qiu Ju at the Shenyang Sports Institute. She was a former Chinese national swordplay champion and had taught me extremely well. I had an excellent grounding in the various practical uses of the sword and the more than twenty different sword techniques. I wondered what more Mei Ying Sheng could teach me. I was soon to find out. According to the introductions to the standard textbooks on 32 sword and 42 sword, there were three basic hand forms: the sword fingers, the left-hand grip and the right hand grip. The latter was used during the greater part of the form. It was described as follows: With the thumb on the inside and the four fingers wrapped around the outside of the handle, techniques could be performed by gripping with the thumb and index finger whilst loosening the other three fingers. The sword could be controlled by exerting pressure with the thumb or by placing the index finger on the hand-guard. This was more or less what Professor Pang and Coach Zhao had taught me. It was all quite simple really, wasn't it?

Master Mei began by saying that *Wu* (舞) was the Chinese character used to describe the action of wielding the sword. Literally this meant to dance, so highlighting the beauty and elegance of its movements. Traditionally there were said to be thirteen different sword techniques - *Jianfa* (剑法) although actually there were more than twenty altogether. Mei Ying Sheng introduced us to an idiom to differentiate between sword and sabre - "*Huo ba jian, Si ba dao*" (活把剑， 死把刀) which meant literally "alive hold the sword, dead hold the sabre." In other words the sabre was rigid and inflexible whereas the sword was lively and flowing. This superior quality could only be imparted by the correct use of the *Jianba* (剑把) - sword grips. "How should we grip the sword?" he asked. "Like this," I said, holding the sword in the way that I had been taught. Master Mei waited. "Any other ways?" he asked. I shook my head. He performed a movement from the form then asked again "How many sword grips did I use?" This time no one answered. "Four," he said. "And that was only one small movement." He continued, "What you showed me was *Luo Ba* (螺把) - the spiralling grip but there are three variations on this grip alone. Just as in tai chi chuan, there is *Yin* palm and *Yang* palm, so in sword there is *Yin jian* - *Yin* sword and *Yang jian* - *Yang* sword. When the right hand holding the sword is palm up, that is *Yang* sword. When the right hand holding the sword is palm down, that is *Yin* sword. And when I turn my wrist completely around so that the upper edge of the sword is facing downwards that is *Fan jian*. The spiralling grip is the most common. However, there are others such as *Man Ba* (满把), *Qian Ba* (钳把), *Ya Ba* (压把) and *Diao Ba* (刁把). Learn their names and how to practise them correctly." Previously I had learned the end result of using the sword - the sword techniques such as chop, cut, point, sweep, parry and so on. However, what I and my teachers had neglected was the means by which the sword was connected to the hand. If this link was weak and faulty, the end technique could not hope to be satisfactorily carried out. Master Mei placed as much emphasis on the way in which the sword was grafted onto the hand as the technique itself. He continued to stress that the sword was an extension of the hand and that the reflection of the movements in the tai chi diagram was equally true in the sword form as in the empty hand form. The shape of the movements themselves or the lines described by the tip of the sword reflected the outline of the black or white fishes in the tai chi diagram. I often sent myself to sleep at night repeating the names of the parts of the fish's body : *Yu Wei* (鱼尾) - fish's tail, *Yu Bei* (鱼背) - fish's back, *Yu Tou* (鱼头) - fish's head, *Yu Duzi* (鱼肚子) - fish's stomach and back to *Yu Wei* (鱼尾) - fish's tail. It was a kind of litany instilled into me by Master Mei. As I practised the form, I would say to myself "*Man ba, Luo ba, Qian ba*" and so on as I deliberately changed from one grip to another. With the sword extended centrally in front of the body, I ensured that the butt was facing down in correct alignment with my lower *Dan Tian*. And I made the tip of the sword dance as it traced the outline of the tai chi diagram. Master Mei had elevated the practice of sword onto a totally different level from the one that I had been accustomed to. No longer was it just another weapon like broadsword, staff and spear, it had become something special. It truly was the prince of weapons in my mind.

The rotation of classes continued. Having learned the traditional short form, Yang style sword and the long 85 step form, we then found ourselves back at the beginning of the cycle again. Having discovered Master Mei on the 20th of June 1993, I didn't finally leave Shenzhen until the 29th of August 1994, by which time I had got married to my Chinese girlfriend Lu Shuo. I suppose that you could say that I served an apprenticeship with Mei Ying Sheng and a courtship with Yang style tai chi. By the end, I had an inseparable relationship with all of them in one way or another. I certainly didn't begin as the star pupil in the class. I struggled like everyone else to come to terms with the refinements of traditional tai chi. In the words of another Chinese idiom "*Zhi Yao Gong Fu Shen, Tie Chu Mo Cheng Zhen*" (只要功夫深，铁杵磨成针) - As long as you work hard, an iron bar can be milled into a needle. In other words, strong will and hard work can achieve everything. I think I took this idiom too literally as I was reduced from twelve stone to ten stone five pounds during my stay in Shenzhen. In Mei Ying Sheng I had a superb role model. I trained hard and practised hard. Over the year I appeared in each rotated class as much as six times. I didn't find the repetition boring and learned something new every time. Besides, by now I had the added responsibility of being Master Mei's number one student. The career of his daughter, Ao Shuang, had taken off and she was frequently away on business so Mei was in need of an experienced student to lead the class and act as his demonstration assistant. I could not have been more proud. However, I did not let my superior status go to my head and kept my feet firmly on the ground. I was affectionately known by Mei Ying Sheng and his class as "*Yang Da Ge*" - foreign big brother. I was happy to be accepted into such a tai chi family.

Our tai chi family was of course part of a much greater tai chi family. The opportunity arose early in 1994 to join ranks with other more distinguished members of that family and with Mei Ying Sheng's teacher, Great Grandmaster Fu Zhong Wen.

A delegation headed by Master Mei set off for Shanghai on Wednesday the 27th April. I was proud to be a member of the party and was the only British person invited to attend. Our purpose was to take part in the Yang style tai chi high level lecture and study class with Master Fu. This occasion formed part of the activities in celebration of the fiftieth anniversary of the founding of the Yongnian Tai Chi Chuan Association of Shanghai. It was a particularly significant event as it brought together three generations of the Fu family, including Master Fu's son, Fu Sheng Yuan and grandson, Fu Qing Quan, who now lived in Australia. As part of the celebration each delegation was offered the opportunity to nominate one of its member to give a display. Master Mei nominated me. I could not have been more proud to demonstrate the Yang style sword form which I had spent so many hours lovingly practising and perfecting. Not only that, for the finale of the whole event there was a mass demonstration of the long 85 step form open only to Chinese delegations. As the official representative of the Shenzhen delegation, I was the only non-Chinese person to take part. My pride gave way to humility as the assembled gathering paid tribute to Great Grandmaster Yang Lu Chan, founder of the Yang family style of tai chi, by observing one minute's silence in remembrance. From one great man to another, Fu Zhong Wen paid tribute to his ancestors and humbly accepted their inheritance of passing on and handing down the treasure that was Yang style tai chi. It was at this moment that I fully appreciated Mei Ying Sheng's selfless commitment to his art. He had been inspired by his master just as I was inspired by him.

By an amazing coincidence at the conclusion of this event on Monday May 2nd, another great event was due to begin in Shanghai the following day. As one door closed, another door opened. This was the World Grand Wushu Festival that took place in Shanghai every two years. Unfortunately there was no special category for traditional Yang style. Nevertheless, on the spur of the moment I decided to take part. I entered two demonstration events: men's tai chi chuan and men's weapons. With Master Mei's approval, I opted for the Yang style tai chi sword form in the latter category and the modern 42 step championship tai chi form in the former category. In this way, I felt that I was representing all my teachers, both those in Shenyang, particularly at the Sports Institute and my traditional master in the figure of Mei Ying Sheng. As a late entry I had to wait my turn and was actually number 44 out of 44 to perform in the men's weapons category. With barely a minute to spare before I had to rush to the airport to catch my plane back to Shenzhen, the chief judge told me that I had won gold medals for outstanding performances in both events. Earlier in the proceeding we had been treated to a group demonstration of the 42 step tai chi form led by men's would champion - Chen Si Tan and women's world champion - Gao Jia Min. Not to be outshone by the youngsters, Fu Zhong Wen reappeared together with the even older 94 year old Master Ma Yue Liang to give a demonstration of traditional tai chi. At the age of 45 as I was at that time, I fell somewhere in the middle and hoped that I still represented some of the vigour of youth with the class and experience of old age.

On my return to Shenzhen, Mei Ying Sheng was delighted with my achievements. Not proud by nature, he couldn't help showing off my gold medals to the class and posing for photographs for the Shenzhen Daily Newspaper. And why not. He deserved the limelight for all the effort he had put into teaching me. I had won the medals for him. It was concrete proof of the excellence of his teaching. Two other opportunities arose to confirm Master Mei's status as a teacher of outstanding quality before I finally left Shenzhen. If a teacher was to be judged by the achievements of his students, then I was determined to do my utmost to promote his status among the ranks.

My status and rank were about to change. I was no longer going to be single. I was getting married. Because my future wife's hometown was Shenyang, we had to return there to get married. I managed to take a few days leave in the middle of June from my job at the Shenzhen College of Education and flew back to the far North of China. I returned to my old room at the guest house of the Shenyang Sports Institute and renewed my acquaintance with my teachers and particularly President Li Le Zheng. That evening President Li invited me to dinner at his house. His wife prepared cow's liver, bull's testicles and strawberries for us. Li Le Zheng and I got drunk on *San Bian Jiu* (三鞭酒) - three whips alcohol. The whips in question were polite words for penis. Apparently the drink was extremely helpful for improving men's virility as it contained deer penis, donkey penis and dog penis. I wasn't sure whether this was a subtle hint that as a man of 45 getting married for the first time, I might need some assistance in the potency stakes. I assured him that I had sufficient reserves of sexual Qi, thank you very much. I drank the stuff anyway. Next day I woke up suffering from a severe case of diarrhoea. I wasn't sure if it was the testicles or the penises. Maybe it was just the good old Shenyang air. In any case, my nether regions had recovered sufficiently to tie the knot at the Public Security Office and immediately fly back to Shenzhen whilst my new wife remained in Shenyang to complete formalities for her to obtain a passport and entry clearance to come to Britain. It may not sound very romantic now but the whole thing was so bizarre that I look back on it with great affection.

Shenzhen was handily located just across the border from Hong Kong. On one of my weekly journeys to the British colony I came across a poster advertising the Hong Kong Open Wushu Championship. I immediately contacted the office of the Hong Kong Wushu Union, spoke to its director Danny Yen and expressed my desire to take part. At first enthusiastic to accept my application, Danny then regrettably informed me that, since I was not a Hong Kong resident but a British citizen living in mainland

China, I wouldn't be able to take part. Thanks to my relentless pleadings he eventually gave in and agreed to accept me in the demonstration event of traditional weapons. It turned out to be quite an event. On Sunday 19th June at the Wai Tsuen Centre I arrived to register at around 9 in the morning. Amazingly I was the only white, non-Chinese competitor out of some 220 entrants. To say that I stuck out like a sore thumb would be an understatement. Dressed in my white silk tai chi suit and brandishing my sword I hung around all day until finally at around 8 p.m. the traditional weapons category got under way. I was number 37 out of 41 competitors so it was well after ten o'clock when I eventually took to the floor. The sense of expectation was overwhelming. I was the only *Gweilo* in front of a knowledgeable Chinese audience. The silence at the beginning of the form and the roar at the end were both deafening. In fact I scored the second highest mark out of the 41 competitors but as it was a demonstration event, those taking part all received medals according to the level of their performance. As mine was in the top level, I received a gold medal. The only other white face present turned out to be a reporter called Kevin Faure from the Hong Kong Daily newspaper, The Eastern Express. He later interviewed me and wrote a half a page spread about me, my master and my tai chi exploits. Later that year Mei Ying Sheng was invited to Hong Kong to teach traditional Yang style tai chi.

During my time in Shenzhen I had made friends with the director of the Shenzhen Sports Association, Chen Xun. She informed me that a large martial arts competition was taking place in Beijing early in August and asked if I would like to enter. Competitions were restricted to three events which made selection difficult. Fortunately there was a traditional Yang style category. This was the Beijing International Wushu and Tai Chi Chuan Invitational Tournament. I was really hoping for the gold medal as at last I would have a platform to show the merits of traditional Yang style tai chi rather that the modern wushu form. As it turned out, I won the bronze medal but was completely satisfied with my performance, receiving the highest individual score from the chief judge. I felt that I had upheld the standards of my Master, Mei Ying Sheng. Incidentally, whilst in Beijing I was able to pick up three copies of the book that I had written in collaboration with Li Le Zheng. This was another concrete sign of my achievements since arriving in China. At long last everything seemed to be crystallising towards a positive conclusion. It was almost time for me to leave.

It is hard to know where to begin to write an appreciation of Master Mei Ying Sheng. He did not know a word of English but he was fluent in the language of tai chi. A good master can show you the way if he himself leads that way in his life. Master Mei Ying Sheng was completely immersed in the traditional art and was untouched by the modern turn of mind. He was totally dedicated to enriching the world through the promotion of what he saw as a pearl of Chinese culture, an inheritance passed down to him by his master who had entrusted him with this priceless gift. In the face of so many competing distractions in the modern world, it is extremely difficult if not impossible to be single-minded in pursuit of one's art. Yet Mei Ying Sheng achieved just that. On the one hand, he was realistic enough to make his art accessible to as many people as possible so that they could enjoy tai chi and derive benefits from it on many different levels. On the other hand, he was able to cultivate a hard core of dedicated students such as myself who shared his unique and undivided love of traditional Yang style tai chi. Before I left Shenzhen I invited Master Mei and his family out to dinner at a restaurant. I presented him with a special tai chi watch I had bought in Hong Kong and a new black silk tai chi suit I had secretly bought in Shanghai. He received these gifts gratefully and graciously but I knew that the best gift I could give him was to continue practising the art that he had so lovingly taught me and to cherish that art as much as he cherished it himself.

WHAT'S IN A NAME?

TEACHER, COACH OR MASTER

A person's title and status in the hierarchy of society in China is of paramount importance. Virtually every professional Chinese person carries a name card which indicates whether he is a president, professor, manager, supervisor, coach, teacher and so on. The Chinese place great emphasis on their relationship to their peers within a work unit or organisation and within society as a whole.

This is equally true of the family structure. Each family member has a particular name which identifies his relationship to every other member. The formal word for father is *Fuqin* (父亲). Informally, I would call my father *Ba* (爸) - a character which contains the radical *Fu* (父) denoting father or male relative. This is the same Fu which is used in the title *Shifu* (师父) meaning master. I would address my grandfather on the paternal side as *Ye* (爷) and on the maternal side as *Lao Ye* (姥爷). *Lao* (老) means old and therefore carries the connotation of respect for the elder generation. It is the same *Lao* as in *Laoshi* which may mean teacher or even master. Note also that the character *Ye* contains within it the radical *Fu*. I would address my father's father, that is my paternal grandfather, as *Tai Ye* (太爷). This is the same *Tai* meaning great as in *Tai Laoshi* meaning (great) grandmaster, and the same *Tai* as in *Tai Ji Quan*. It can thus be seen that there is a great deal of overlap between those terms used within the family and the martial arts hierarchy.

The structure of traditional martial arts training is akin to that of a family. At the top, one has the oldest, most revered members who nowadays in the field of Yang style tai chi would represent the fourth generation inheritance of the family line. Their sons would represent the fifth generation of Yang style teachers and their sons' sons the sixth generation. By way of example, until his untimely death on the 24th of September 1994, Fu Zhong Wen, the doyen of Yang style tai chi in China, was a fourth generation master; his son Fu Sheng Yuan a fifth generation master; and his grandson Fu Qing Quan a sixth generation master. In the West, we would probably address them as follows : Fu Zhong Wen as Great Grandmaster, Fu Sheng Yuan as Grandmaster and Fu Qing Quan as Master.

However, in China it is not so simple or clear-cut. There are no direct and straightforward equivalents in Chinese. In fact it would be possible to address them all as *Laoshi* (老师). If one really wanted to draw a distinction between them, one could address the grandfather as *Tai Laoshi*, the father as *Shifu* and the son as *Laoshi*. However, even this would not represent the definitive form of address as it does not take into account the status of the person who is speaking. On a personal level, I would address Fu Zhong Wen as *Tai Laoshi* as he is my master's teacher and is one generation older than him. I would address my master, Mei Ying Sheng as *Laoshi*. I would also address Fu Sheng Yuan as *Laoshi* because he is of the same generation as my master and they share the same teacher. According to custom, I should address Fu Qing Quan as *Shi Di* (师弟) meaning teacher little brother as his father, Fu Sheng Yuan, is of the same status as my master, and I am older than him. An individual's title and form of address depend on his position in the tai chi family tree, on his status as perceived by his peers and the respective rank of the person addressing him.

Titles carry with them many inherent attributes. At this juncture, it may be useful to examine the history and significance of some of the forms of address often applied to tai chi masters, namely *Laoshi, Shifu, Da Shi* and *Tai Shi*. The first point to be noted is the character of *Shi* (师) which is common to all these titles. This character dates back to the Tang Dynasty when a famous poet, Han Yu (韩愈) wrote a celebrated article on the subject of *Shi*. The first sentence of this article is the definition of the character *Shi* itself : *Shizhe , Chuandao, Shouye, Jie Huo, Zhe Ye* (师者，传道、授业、解惑者也) - Teaching, passing on, conferring professional skills,explaining puzzles. As far as the form of address of *Laoshi* is concerned, this dates back some two thousand years and was used to refer to all knowledgeable people who possessed skills and who handed these skills on to others. In the Han Dynasty, a famous writer/historian called Si Ma Qian produced a work entitled *Shi Ji* (A Record of History) in which the eldest, most learned people were referred to as *Laoshi*. Nowadays in China, teachers in universities, high schools and junior schools are all called *Laoshi*. Teachers of wushu in Sports Institutes and at city, provincial and national team level are *Jiaolian* (教练) - Coaches by profession. However, their title for purposes of address would still be *Laoshi*.

Shifu is probably the most widely used form of address for a master, particularly in the West where it is often shortened to "Sifu". However, it should be recognized that in Chinese the word *Shifu* may be written in two distinct ways (师父 and 师傅) and has two distinct meanings, although today they have become more or less interchangeable. In ancient times they both meant *Laoshi*. Both forms contain the identical character *Shi* as in *Laoshi* but the character for *Fu* is different. One *Fu* (父) means father. The other *Fu* (傅) means teaching, guiding and distributing skills. In Buddhism, the monks addressed their teachers as either *Shifu* (师父) or *Shifu* (师傅) because they regarded their teachers as their fathers, and their teachers were also responsible for their spiritual guidance. The field of martial arts and tai chi in particular entailed treating your teacher as a father figure and submitting oneself to his guidance in the acquisition of skills. There was over history a gradual shift to the use of *Shifu* (师父) partly for the simple reason that this character was easier to write. In addition, the change from *Shifu* (师傅) to *Shifu* (师父) had an historical reason. During the process of teaching, the relationship between teacher and disciple or student was based strongly on mutual reliance. In Chinese culture, loyalty and respect for parent figures received much attention.Therefore, if you called your teacher *Shifu* (师父), you accorded your teacher the same status as your father. After Liberation, the title *Shifu* (师父), although not officially banned by the government, actually disappeared for the most part from common usage.It was supplanted by *Shifu* (师傅) as the Communist Party believed that there should be equality between teachers and students, masters and disciples or apprentices. Therefore, the relationship between teacher and student should not be like father and son. In the 1950's and 1960's, the title *Shifu* (师傅) was used. During the Cultural Revolution, there was a call in the "Thoughts of Chairman Mao" for the working class to take the lead in all areas. Thus *Shifu* (师傅) became the most respectful and fashionable form of address throughout China.

Martial arts followed the tradition of any other profession in distributing its skills. Behind closed doors, students continued to call their teachers *Shifu* (师父). After Liberation, private martial arts organizations were banned and martial arts was listed as a sports event. It became a formal subject in Sports Institutes and special sports schools. As a result, at this point all martial arts teachers had to be addressed as *Laoshi* as they were regarded as coaches - *Jiaolian* (教练) and not masters. In spite of this restriction, in private students still called their aged and most respected martial arts seniors *Shifu* (师父). Those who teach in Sports Institutes nowadays have their formal professional titles such as professor, assistant professor or lecturer. In this context no one is addressed as *Shifu*. They are all addressed in general speech as *Laoshi*. However, in line with China's open-door policy, in the past four or five years on the mainland, many private schools have sprung up and are flourishing. As a result, *Shifu* has been resumed as a form of address in some domestic situations and you are basically free to address your teacher as you or he sees fit and appropriate.

It is important to mention at this stage that there is a difference between mainland China, Taiwan, Hong Kong and overseas Chinese usage in general. This is mainly due to the Cultural Revolution. Notably, the change in the status of *Shifu* refers to mainland China. It does not apply to overseas Chinese territories. In mainland China under the guidance of Marxism and Leninism it was considered that the relationship between teacher and student as one of father and son was a symbol of feudalism. It was regarded as the expression of an outdated, backward way of thinking. On the other hand, outside mainland China the form of address of *Shifu* has never really disappeared.

There exist forms of address higher than *Laoshi* or *Shifu*. *Da Shi* (大师)is derived from the more ancient title of *Tai Shi* (太师). *Da* means big and *Tai* means great and old. In ancient times, *Tai Shi* (太师), *Tai Fu* (太傅) and *Tai Bao* (太保) were the highest ranks. In the field of martial arts, the titles *Zushi* (祖师) and *Zushiye* (祖师爷) refer to the inventor or founder of a certain style. The character *Zu* means ancestor or originator. The character *Ye* means grandfather or is a form of address for someone of an older generation. Grandmaster and Great Grandmaster may be translated as *Tai Shi*. *Tai Shi* refers to an individual who has attained especially highly acknowledged outstanding achievements in the field of martial arts after many years of practice, dedication, scholarship and endeavour. A time element is required in order to reach this status. On the other hand, *Zu Shi (Ye)* refers to the inventor of a school of martial arts, whether he is alive or dead. In recent history, those aged and revered masters who excelled in certain skills or academic subjects were referred to as *Da Shi*. Nowadays in China it is the government and the respective governing bodies which authorize the conferring of such titles. In the area of martial arts, the government has never bestowed the title of *Da Shi* on an individual master. This does not, however, prevent followers of a certain master from addressing him as *Da Shi* or more commonly as *Tai Sh*i if he is extremely aged and revered. In order to receive the officially authorized title of *Tai Shi* or *Da Shi*, the master must have fulfilled certain requirements. In pre-Liberation times, he had to have been the champion in various national competitions, to have served as the bodyguard to the Emperor or other high-ranking officials, to have had his fighting skills acknowledged as the greatest, or to have had many disciples, all of whom were outstanding martial arts practitioners in their own right. Nowadays in China in order to be officially recognized, a master must have an outstanding reputation based on the excellence of his technique, his contribution to his art in the form of learned articles, treatises and books, and the teaching of large numbers of students throughout China and also abroad.

As far as my own master, Mei Ying Sheng is concerned, he fulfills all of the above criteria. He is a retired doctor of medicine, a surgeon and acupuncturist. He has studied the art of tai chi for more than forty years under fourth and fifth generation masters such as Fu Zong Wen, Gu Liu Xin and Li Zi Yi. He is a permanent member of the Chinese National Fellowship of Taijiquan.In I983 he was awarded the title of the outstanding national martial arts instructor by the Chinese National Wushu Association. He is a member of the Council of the China Yongnian International Tai Chi Association, which is the governing body for traditional Yang style in China. He has devised and had accepted by the above body a short traditional Yang style routine. In the last twenty years Mei Ying Sheng has taught more than thirteen thousand students, of whom the best have won gold medals in international competitions. Since 1995 he has been a member of the editorial staff of the magazine "Zhonguo Taijiquan" and has had original articles published in "Zhonguo Wushu", "Wushu Jian Shen", "Zhonguo Taijiquan", "Wu Lin",the American magazine "Tai Chi", "Combat", "Fighting Arts International" and many others in Taiwan and Hong Kong. Originally from Le Shan in Sichuan Province, Mei Ying Sheng is now resident in Shenzhen, a special economic zone in Guangdong Province where he teaches twice daily in Lizi Park. From the very beginnning I addressed him formally as *Mei Laoshi*, although it would also be possible to address him as *Mei Daifu* (梅大夫) - Dr Mei because of his medical qualifications.

From my own personal experiences, there would appear to be a discrepancy between the north and south of China. In the south of China, principally Guangdong Province as well as in Hong Kong and Taiwan, *Shifu* is an acceptable form of address for a martial arts teacher. However, in the north it is not acceptable due to its usage in everyday Chinese amongst ordinary working people. You would address someone who held a very menial job with extremely low social status as *Shifu* in order to boost his self-esteem especially if you required his attention or you wanted him to do something for you. On my first meeting with Liu You Zhen, the Senior Coach of the Liaoning Province Wushu Team, who were the 1991 national champions, I addressed her as "*Shifu*". She had been assigned to me by the Liaoning Province Sports Commission as my personal tai chi coach. As one of the elite coaches in the north-east of China, I wanted to make a good impression on her. I presumed that I was according her the full dignity of her senior status, when in fact I was addressing her as the lowest of the low. She was absolutely horrified and told me to call her "*Liu Laoshi*". This was my first encounter with the minefield of forms of address. I made sure that I got it right from then on.

STUDENT, APPRENTICE OR DISCIPLE

In old China as far back as the Tang Dynasty (618-907) if you wanted to learn a particular skill, there was no professional school that you could attend. You had to act as an apprentice and place yourself in the hands of a master (*Shifu*). Apprenticeships were hard to come by and fiercely sought after - sometimes as low as one and certainly no more than five. When you became an apprentice, your *Shifu* supplied you with accommodation, food and clothing but no salary. In return, you would simply work in your master's house. Normally, in the first two years you would not learn any skills at all. This period simply served to establish your worthiness to be accepted as an apprentice. There is an old saying in Chinese *Xue Tu, Xue Tu, San Nian Wei Nu* (学徒，学徒，三年为奴) - Apprentice, apprentice, three years as a slave. The *Shifu* were worried that their apprentices might become better craftsman than themselves and so adversely affect their own businesses. Another Chinese idiom serves to illustrate this fear : *Jiao Hui Liao Tu Di, E Si Liao Shifu* (教会了徒弟，饿死了师傅) - After the disciples have completed their learning, the master will go hungry. However, the idiom which best sums up and epitomizes the relationship between a master and his apprentice or disciple goes as follows : *Yi Ri Wei Shi, Zhong Sheng Wei Fu* (一日为师，终生为父) - One day as a teacher, the whole life as a father. In other words, if you act as my teacher for only one day, for the rest of my life you will be my father. This idiom both reflects the old Chinese tradition of respecting your teacher and the importance of obedience in Chinese culture.

The integrity of the relationship between a teacher and his student or a master and his disciple is at the heart of how deeply you may train in your chosen art. This is particularly true in the case of tai chi. Let us firstly try to clarify some of the terms used in martial arts to refer to a student or disciple. The usual word for student is *Xuesheng* (学生) which simply denotes a person who has learned or studied a particular branch of knowledge. *Xuetu* (学徒) does mean apprentice and the word *Tudi* (徒弟) does mean follower or disciple. However, the most appropriate title to refer to a tai chi disciple is *Dizi* (弟子) which contains the character *Di* (弟) meaning little brother, so reinforcing the belief that anyone becoming the disciple of a master is in effect being accepted as a member of the family. Not only that, but the disciple agrees to take his master as his father and follow and obey him for the rest of his life. An even closer disciple would be the *Bai Men Dizi* (拜门弟子) - the indoor/inside disciple which involves undergoing the process of *Bai Shi* (拜师). *Bai Shi* is a ceremony of acceptance which is still followed today by some masters. The disciple in question must have developed a certain advanced level of skill, displayed a high moral character and shown respect for his master and dedication to his art. The *Bai Shi* may take the form of a quasi-religious ceremony at which incense is burned and during which an oath of lifetime allegiance and obedience is sworn to the master and his ancestors. This may be accompanied by the disciple drawing blood from his finger which is then mixed with wine and drunk. It is reminiscent of the ritual of *Bai Bai* (拜拜) performed by initiates into Buddhism when they clasp hands, bow and pay homage to their deity.

Not all masters believe in or follow the initiation of *Bai Shi* for their closest students. My master, Mei Ying Sheng, sincerely believes in an open policy of teaching the complete system of traditional Yang style tai chi to any student who is willing to dedicate his time and energies to learning and practising diligently. Of course, in practice such people are few and far between. Even in China most people practise for half an hour two or three times a week. I studied with Master Mei twice a day every day for more than a year and practised five or six hours a day. The bond formed during this period ensured that I effectively took him as my master and he accepted me as his disciple. This was an extended apprenticeship and initiation built on mutual respect and trust. When I first joined his class I was regarded with a certain novelty value by my fellow students. Mei Ying Sheng was assisted by his wife and daughter and senior student, Chi Hui. At first I took my place on the back rank and blended in with the others. As I learned more and my confidence grew, I appeared on the front rank more frequently. A special short form, the long 85 step form and tai chi sword were taught in rotation with sabre only occasionally being studied. To give some idea of the extent and length of my study, over the year I figured in six different classes of Yang style tai chi sword. By the half year point I was established as Master Mei's number one student not only in his eyes but also in the eyes of my fellow students. As he instructed, I would lead the class or act as his partner for demonstration purposes. In his absence, I would take the class myself and other students would defer to me as the senior student, regardless of the fact that I was a foreigner. Whereas I was previously known by my Chinese name of *Tuo Ma Si* (托马斯), I eventually became known in the group by the name Master Mei gave me *Yang Da Ge* (洋大哥) meaning foreign big brother. Training and discussion were not confined to our pitch in Lizhi Park. On Saturday and Sunday mornings in particular after class we would retire to the restaurant on the edge of the park for morning tea and dimsums and continue our discussions on the finer points of tai chi for several hours. In the afternoons Master Mei would retire to his apartment to pursue his research and write articles on various aspects of traditional Yang style tai chi. As a retired doctor, he was especially interested in the medical and health aspects of tai chi - a feature which influenced his entire approach to his art and to his teaching. I would join him for in-depth discussions. We would pour over rare Chinese tai chi books and minutely study the works and photographs of his teachers. In all the time that I knew Mei Ying Sheng, he never talked about anything other than tai chi. He was the epitome of complete dedication to his art.

In May 1994 Mei Ying Sheng led a delegation from Shenzhen to Shanghai to celebrate the fiftieth anniversary of the founding of the Yongnian Taijiquan Association of Shanghai by Great Grandmaster Fu Zhong Wen. Delegations attended from all over the world - the USA, Canada, Australia, Japan, Taiwan, Malaysia, Indonesia as well as representatives from cities throughout China. The celebration took the form of a high level lecture and study class involving three generations of the Fu family : Fu Zhong Wen himself, his son Fu Sheng Yuan, and his grandson Fu Qing Quan. The Saturday afternoon was given over to tai chi weapons training. Master Fu invited a representative from each delegation to give a demonstration. Without hesitation Mei Ying Sheng appointed me to represent the delegation from Shenzhen. I was overcome with a deep sense of pride that Master Mei should nominate me to represent him and it served to confirm that in his eyes I was his number one student and disciple even though I was a foreigner. It was a great honour. Master Fu handed me his own sword and although a little nervous at first, I completed the traditional long Yang style sword form filled with a sense of euphoria to have taken part in this historic occasion. The climax of the whole fiftieth anniversary event took place in the main auditorium of Shanghai's Tong Ji University. After several rounds of presentations, eulogies and speeches, Fu Zhong Wen himself rose to speak. He concluded by stating that his lifetime's dedication to the promotion of traditional Yang style tai chi had been a pleasure and was a reward in itself. It was not necessary to praise him for simply doing something that was his duty and a debt of honour that he owed to his master, Yang Cheng Fu and his ancestors. We all stood in silence for one minute in remembrance of Yang Lu Chang, Great Grandmaster and founder of the Yang family style of tai chi. It was at this moment when such a great man as Fu Zhong Wen paid tribute with such sincere humility and reverence to his teachers that I fully understood what constituted the fundamentals of the master/disciple relationship. This moment crystallized all the arguments theorizing about family, hierarchy, titles and forms of address. You only had to look at how a person conducted his life through his art to recognise that he was a true master. Back in the auditorium the proceedings continued with a series of demonstrations on the stage. Fu Qing Quan gave a performance of tai chi broadsword. There then followed a bout of moving push hands between Fu Zhong Wen and Fu Sheng Yuan which drew delighted applause from the audience to see the old master in such sprightly form. Next it was the turn of the Chinese representatives of the Yongnian Association to give a mass performance of traditional Yang style tai chi. It was stressed that this was strictly for representatives from within China and was not open to foreign guests from abroad. As I was resident in China and was representing the Chinese city of Shenzhen and not Great Britain, Master Mei told me to go up on stage. Much to the amazement and amusement of the crowd, I took my place on the first rank and led the Chinese delegates in a demonstration of the long 85 step form.What a great experience and one that I shall always treasure. An uplifting finale to a truly historic occasion.

So far I have only examined the positive aspects of studying with a Chinese master. Just as it is an extremely important step for a master to accept you as a disciple, it is equally vital for you to find the right master. Making the wrong choice and selecting an unsuitable or unworthy teacher can have disastrous results. For a while I studied with a certain tai chi master and experienced some of the downside of being a foreign student. Although I do not wish to appear ungrateful and am very thankful for the hospitality he showed in accepting me into his family, I feel that I should point out some of the pitfalls and dangers of becoming attached to a particular teacher who may not be as humble, selfless and highly principled as Mei Ying Sheng. I also share the blame for allowing myself to be used as a pawn in a power game. It is just as important for a student to choose his master wisely as it is for him to be accepted by his master.

The basic flaw lay in this master's perception of me as his student. After a while I gained the impression that he regarded me as his property and would show me off to his fellow masters who did not have a foreign student of their own. A master was judged not only by the number and calibre of his students but also by his ability to attract foreign students. To have a foreigner under your guidance gave you additional kudos. So he would use me to boost his standing amongst his peers. If we went out as a group to the restaurant, he would use his supposed powers of *qi* against me. Not wishing to offend and not wishing to make him lose face, I complied with his little charades. However, these faked manifestations of *qi* power only served to diminish him in my eyes. Eventually I managed to contrive an honourable withdrawal from his clique. But I learned a salutary lesson. The professional jealousy of his fellow masters did little to impress me either. On leaving the master's apartment, I was sometimes accosted by the other masters who invited me to their homes, plied me with alcohol, showed off their skills and told me that they would teach me their innermost secrets if I would become their disciple and follower. Needless to say, I declined their invitations even though I was sorely tempted to acquire the skills they had offered me. How could I honour and obey such unscrupulous teachers? How could I take them as my father? The relationship between a master and his student should be built on mutual respect and trust, not on the desire for self-aggrandizement on the one hand and a selfish desire to obtain secret skills cheaply on the other hand.

The integrity of the student-master relationship is sacrosanct. It cannot be bought or acquired cheaply but should develop, be nurtured and cherished naturally over an extended period of time, during which the student earns the master's trust and good faith. Mei Ying Sheng never held back from teaching me all he knew. He was totally secure in the integrity of his own knowledge and skills. Only the insecure teacher is frightened of having his authority usurped and his skills surpassed by his students and deliberately holds back from passing on his ultimate secrets and skills. Master Mei would chastize me if I ever said that I would never be as good as him. He insisted that I should aim to equal if not better his standards. A student or disciple should firstly attempt to follow in his footsteps and emulate his master. But he should ultimately seek to surpass him. Otherwise the inheritance of tai chi would gradually be dissipated and diluted generation by generation. A student's aim should be to set even higher goals and achieve even higher standards than his master.

To illustrate the entirely selfless nature of a master like Mei Ying Sheng and his desire for me to learn as much as possible during my stay in China, I should like to cite one example.After nearly a year, and about two months before I was due to return to England, I felt that apart from my devotion to traditional Yang style tai chi, I should like to keep up my practice of Chen style. I already knew the 56 step international competition form and the old style traditional first form which I had learned from

Guan Tie Yun at the Shenyang Sports Institute. I dearly wanted to learn the traditional Chen style sword form. After training with Master Mei I had acquired a particular affection for the sword. I already knew the standard 32 sword form, the 42 competition sword form, Bagua sword and Yang style sword. There was an outstanding coach in Lizhi Park in Shenzhen called Li Xiao Ling. She had studied Chen style in the Chen village with Chen Zhen Lei and was the 1992 Chinese national ladies Chen style tai chi champion. She was organizing a class on Chen style tai chi sword and I wished to enrol. This placed me in a considerable dilemma. I approached Master Mei, informed him of my wish and asked him if he would have any objection. Deep down inside I have to say that I felt like a traitor, asking him for permission to train with another teacher, even if only temporarily. Master Mei could not have been more magnanimous. He perceived my unease and quickly put my mind at rest. There was not even the slightest trace of professional jealousy. He gave his complete blessing. What is more, he actively encouraged me to study with other teachers. To his mind, any knowledge I gained from whatever source was useful. His reaction was in sharp contrast to my earlier experience with the other master and his companions. Master Mei's humility and dignity showed me that here was a real master whose conduct and entire code of ethics were a credit to the art which he so dearly cherished.

For a while after meeting Mei Ying Sheng I had completely abandoned everything I had previously learned at the Shenyang Sports Institute. I regarded the modern, recently devised competition forms in Yang, Chen, Wu and Sun as pale imitations of traditional tai chi. The 42 step tai chi and tai chi sword championship routines had been cobbled together by committees of masters and lacked the unique flavour of any one family style. However, after a period of reflexion, I concluded that it would be a terrible pity to give up something that I had spent so long acquiring, practising and perfecting. So it was that my enthusiasm for the modern forms was renewed. I wanted to continue to practise the new tai chi routines and I wanted to learn something different just to stimulate me and prevent me from getting stale through the daily practice of the same few routines. So it was that I entered Li Xiao Ling's Chen style tai chi sword class. As with Master Mei, I began at the back, gradually worked my way to the front and eventually became Coach Li's number one student, class leader and demonstrator. Barely a stone's throw away from our training pitch, I could see Mei Ying Sheng continuing to teach his class. From time to time we would catch each other's eye and exchange a knowing glance. I realized that although I was temporarily in another teacher's class, I was still his student. The fact that I excelled in another teacher's group was a reflection on how well he had taught me.

The relationship between a teacher and his student, a master and his disciple is complex, subtle and bound up in many cultural traits and Chinese traditions in which the family plays a central role. Knowledge of the art of a specific family system of tai chi was originally held as a closely guarded family secret. It was handed down from father to son or to the number one student. In view of this tradition of privilege and secrecy, potential students had first to demonstrate their respect and dedication before being considered eligible to be taken on by a master at all. The highest levels of knowledge of a system would only be passed on to the master's sons or most senior students on condition that they had earned that privilege on merit. If no one individual demonstrated this extreme worth, then the master would not divulge these secrets and would die without passing them on. Thankfully nowadays modern masters take a more pragmatic approach. They may still be selective about whom they choose to be their closest students and disciples. But the necessity to ensure that the Chinese national treasure that is tai chi will survive and prosper far outweighs the allegiance to family and secrecy.

The oral tradition of handing down skills in the field of tai chi is still prevalent today and derives from the fact that many famous masters never wrote a single book, article or treatise on their art. They did not bequeath a written legacy, just a few sketches and perhaps some faded black and white photographs. This accounts for the scarcity of written material both on the family systems and the history of tai chi itself. This regrettable omission does on the one hand lend the art of tai chi a certain mystique and inaccessibility. On the other hand, it makes the task of the tai chi scholar, archivist and historian extremely difficult. The lack of documentation is being compensated for by the efforts of present day masters such as Mei Ying Sheng who commit their own thoughts to paper as well as the remembered teachings of their own masters. It is vitally important for the future of tai chi that this legacy be fully documented and recorded for the benefit of future generations both in Chinese and translated into the other major languages of the world.

It could be argued that tai chi is such a profound, abstruse subject that to write a complete account of its art would be an impossible task. Besides, the art of tai chi cannot be learned from a book. At the highest levels, the constraints of language defy even a master's gifts of language to express something which may only be developed and experienced at first hand. The role of the teacher-student/master-disciple relationship cannot be overemphasized. This is an age when magazines are full of advertisements for books and videotapes promising to teach the secrets of the masters. These are empty promises. Nothing can match or take the place of the oral tradition of the art and infinite skills of tai chi. Nothing can approach in depth of experience the unique bond of a disciple and his master.

TAI CHI AS A SPORT OR AN ART

FISH OR BEAR'S PAW

Everyone has an image in his own mind of what tai chi is. However, this image has many different reflections - some of them clear and some of them distorted. My tai chi journey was rather like walking down a hall of mirrors. Sometimes my tai chi reflection was short and fat. Sometimes it was tall and thin. I could also draw the analogy of tai chi being like a chameleon, constantly changing its colour in order to blend in with its background. The fact that it is a rather slippery creature like a character from "Alice in Wonderland" makes it all the more alluring as it can never be tamed or pinned down. It always seems to defy perfect definition.

It is therefore extremely difficult to classify tai chi and place it in one specific category. Is it a sport or is it an art? On the one hand, modern wushu tai chi as seen in competitions is a sport. In Chinese it would be described as *Tiyu Yundong* (体育运动) - a sports event. On the other hand, traditional tai chi as practised by family style masters is regarded as an art. In Chinese it would be described as *Yishu* (艺术) - art or skill. Are these two branches of tai chi mutually exclusive or can they co-exist and even overlap? What exactly are the criteria that are applied to define tai chi as either a sport or an art? And are these the only two possible definitions of tai chi, or are there others?

The beauty of tai chi is that it is genuinely all things to all people. It is at one and the same time a competitive sport, a martial art, a form of moving meditation, a tool for healing and health promotion and purely and simply an art(form). The apparent contradiction is that it can be all these things at the same time in different people's eyes. It simply depends which mirrors you are looking in. The problem I had in China was that it was difficult to look in more than one mirror at a time.

There is a Chinese proverb: *Er Zhe Bu Ke Jian De, She Yu Er Qu Xiong Zhang Zhe Ye.* (二者不可兼得，舍鱼而取熊掌者也) which means you cannot have at the same time both fish and bear's paw. In other words, you must choose between two equally desirable alternatives. At first I had studied modern tai chi competition forms which I loved. Then I came across a traditional Yang style tai chi master who opened up my eyes to the true potential of tai chi as an art. At first I completely abandoned my Sports Institute training and international championship tai chi routines. After a while I thought to myself that it was a terrible waste to discard what I had spent so much time and energy acquiring and so began to practise these routines once more. I have to admit that at the time I felt guilty as I knew that my master thoroughly disapproved of and even despised these modern manifestations of tai chi designed by committees and promoted as just another sports event rather than being cherished as a Chinese national treasure. I just had to learn to live with this guilt but I certainly took on board the necessity to rid myself of many of the forms I had learned early on in my stay in China. I had fallen into the trap that befalls all foreigners. They want to learn everything! This acquisitiveness means that you know many things superficially and nothing substantially. You simply carry around with you a great deal of excess baggage which weighs you down and prevents you from finding enlightenment. The less you know, the better you can know it.

The increasing popularity of tai chi both at home and abroad has posed several problems and has even created some new problems. The national body responsible for promoting and popularising tai chi is the Chinese State Commission for Physical Culture and Sport. With the founding of the People's Republic of China in 1949, steps were taken to preserve and propagate China's cultural heritage. This included the rich and varied field of wushu - Chinese martial arts. The first step came in 1956 when a simplified set of tai chi in 24 forms was devised, loosely based on the sequences of Yang Cheng Fu's family style. Since then, other more comprehensive routines in 48 and 88 forms have been compiled together with a 32 step tai chi sword form. The object was to make tai chi more standardised and accessible to the public at large. The danger in so doing was that the art became devalued and diluted and the essential tenets, precepts and values of tai chi were compromised. In the foreword to their book "Tai Chi 48 Forms and Swordplay" compiled by the China Sports Editorial Board, the editors describe the 24 step form as "having gained widespread popularity both at home and abroad as a means of keeping fit." The 48 forms routine was devised in order to "raise their technical standard further by learning something more demanding" and "containing more complicated movements and involving greater physical exertion." The inference to be drawn from this is that the State Commission for Physical Culture and Sport viewed tai chi primarily as a sporting activity which could be instrumental in raising people's fitness level.

To throw tai chi even more clearly into the spotlight, it had to be seen on the international stage as a competitive sport. With this in mind, the 42 step international tai chi boxing and tai chi sword forms were devised. These events now play a prominent part in national wushu championships, the Asian Games and the World Wushu Championships. As such, the State Commission has to be applauded for raising the profile of tai chi on the world stage. But at what price? In the introduction to Xie Shou De's English version of "International Wushu Competition Routines" it states that "Wushu, as an international competitive sport, is truly developing on a world-wide scale in leaps and bounds. There is an urgent need to standardise wushu competition routines in order that Chinese and foreign competitors may compete on an equal footing." Tai chi chuan was one of the seven disciplines to be selected for standardisation. Standardisation and the necessity to conform with international wushu competition rules gave rise to an end product that was a compromise, devised by a select group of masters, coaches and professors. Apart from the Yang style elements, the 42 form also contains movements taken from the three other principal styles of tai chi in mainland China - Chen, Wu and Sun. However, because the hybrid routine blends several styles, there is no purity or uniformity of movement. This detracts from the beauty and integrity of the original traditional styles and results in a form lacking in unique spirit, style and flavour. It would appear that they had successfully created a sport but destroyed an art.

In order to redress the balance and to counteract the above shortcomings, competition forms in the four main styles were devised. First published in 1989 by the People's Sports Publishing House of China and approved by the Chinese Wushu Association, the book "Competition Routines for Four Styles Tijiquan" appeared in print. It included the 40 Yang style form devised by Zhang Wen Guang, the 56 Chen style, the 45 Wu style and the 73 Sun style forms. In the foreword to this book, the compilers admitted to the previous "Lack of uniformity in the content and structure of the routines" and stated that there existed "An urgent need to standardise taijiquan routines in order to interflow and develop taijiquan internationally. The consensus of opinion was that these routines, while retaining the traditional characteristic features, embody higher degrees of difficulty in technical execution, which is good for raising the standard of the sport and for competition." One is therefore left with the distinct impression that tai chi is viewed as a valuable product to be packaged and marketed for international consumption. It is openly labelled as a sport, and a competitive sport at that, which can only differentiate between different levels of attainment by increasing the level of technical difficulty. No mention at all is made here of internal content.

With particular regard to Yang style, the compilers continued, "The Yang style routine is based mainly on the writings of Yang Cheng Fu, the founder of this style, with some minor modifications. Thus the new routine includes a Pat Foot movement which is not found in the traditional exercise. Also, a higher degree of difficulty is imposed on the Kick With Heel and Kick to Both Sides movements in which the foot must be brought up to a level higher than the waist. The movements of the whole routine are reasonably arranged according to practical needs of attack and defence, while bringing out the soft, flowing style of the Yang school." In traditional Yang style tai chi there are only three kinds of kicks. *Deng Jiao* (蹬脚) - Kick With The Heel, *Fen Jiao* (分脚) - Separate the Foot and *Bai Lian* (摆莲) - Lotus Kick. The addition of *Pai Jiao* (拍脚) - Slap the Foot is a concession to the compulsory competition tai chi forms which must contain four kicks.

Far from being the consensus of opinion that these forms retain traditional characteristic features, most traditional family style tai chi masters hold strong reservations about the authenticity of these newly devised routines. Master Mei Ying Sheng is of the opinion that if one scrutinizes the fixed postures of Yang Cheng Fu's tai chi and compares them with those of the 40 forms Yang style competition routine, there are in fact very few similarities. Mei Ying Sheng is not alone in his reservations. Noted scholar Professor Zhi Jun wrote that the external appearance of the new championship routines is contrary to the essential characteristics of tai chi chuan. To the untrained eye, adding a kick and deviating from precisely held postures is of no great concern. It may seem an insignificant matter but it is symptomatic of how traditional tai chi is being eroded for the sake of its promotion as a competitive sporting event.

Fortunately powers are at work on behalf of the promotion of pure traditional tai chi as an art. Associations exist whose declared aim is to maintain the standards and popularize the practice of traditional family style tai chi. Notable among these organisations is the Yongnian Taijiquan Association of Shanghai founded by Fu Zhong Wen and the China Yongnian International Taijiquan Association. Since 1991 the latter has organised a biennial gathering in Handan City Yongnian County, Hebei Province - the hometown of the founder of Yang style, Yang Lu Chan. In 1993, there were 1,500 representatives of 152 tai chi organisations from 21 countries. 1995's gathering was on an even grander scale and 1997 promises to surpass even this. In addition, individual masters such as Yang Zhen Duo, Chen Xiao Wang and Fu Sheng Yuan have been instrumental in promoting tai chi in Europe, the United States and Australia.

The question is how far can the bounds of tai chi be pushed in terms of technical difficulty for competition purposes. The difficulty level is to a large extent increased according to how high a competitor can kick. The requirement is currently above waist height but most top level competitors already achieve at least chest height with effortless ease. Future requirements will probably stipulate head height but what then? One of my tai chi teachers, Li Xiao Ling, was able to kick incredibly high, well above head height. This was an amazing feat. However, it went beyond the point where it was graceful and aesthetically pleasing and could not be focused on a specific target point. This begs the questions: Is this an accurate criterion for judging the difficulty of a routine? High kicking requires stretching your hamstrings. A gymnast with little or no previous training in tai chi could probably score quite highly if high kicks, low stances and deep postures were the only competitive criteria. Is this a satisfactory state of affairs? Tai chi exponents with 20 years or more of experience and approaching middle age may be in their tai chi prime but cannot hope to compete in purely physical terms with their younger counterparts.

One only has to look at the kind of competitor taking part in the Chinese National Tai Chi Championships to see that this trend is already happening to a certain extent. An average competitor would be characterised as young (about 20), tall, slim, good-looking and relatively inexperienced in tai chi terms. (Perhaps it is symptomatic of China's headlong rush into modernism and consumerism with an accompanying disintegration of its traditional family values and a lack of reverence for that which is old.) Paradoxically it would appear to be foreign practitioners of tai chi who are more concerned with preserving the traditions of old family style tai chi than the Chinese themselves. You only have to look at the list of events in competitions to see this. In the Chinese National Wushu Championships the only tai chi chuan events are the 42 empty hand and sword forms. There is not even a place for the individual styles competition forms. At the Chinese National Tai Chi Championships, which you would assume to be the home of tradition, there is no place at all for traditional forms. Those examined are only the newly devised competition forms. This is a sad and scandalous state of affairs. In contrast, take any major tai chi tournament in Europe and America, and you will find that traditional tai chi as well as traditional forms of other events take equal status with their modern wushu conterparts in the events schedule.

The esteem in which the events are held can also be judged by the choice of venues. In 1992 when I attended the Chinese National Tai Chi Championships, they took place in the small provincial town of Jinzhou. There was no national publicity. The event was poorly attended and was not covered by the national or even regional media. Even in the town itself, no one seemed to know that it was taking place. I had real difficulty finding the venue. What I assumed to be an extremely prestigious national event took place in a run-down, dusty and dimly-lit railway athletic sports hall. And the event which should have lasted five days was curtailed to three due to lack of funds. I was thoroughly embarrassed and downhearted by this sorry state of affairs. Contrast this with the events organised in Europe and America which take place in prominent locations in big cities in five star hotels and conference centres. Interestingly enough, international events in China such as the Beijing International Wushu and Taijiquan Invitational Tournament which I attended in 1994 command prime locations and are shown live on CCTV. The Beijing Tournament was held on the magnificent site of the eleventh Asian Games and the events took place in the Olympic Stadium. This makes the neglect and lack of support for domestic tai chi events all the more depressing. It is to be hoped that in future similar prominence and financial backing will be given to Chinese National Tai Chi Championships, despite the fact that no foreigners take part and there are no opportunities to stage spectacular international set pieces to impress the Olympic Selection Committee.

It could be argued that the martial side of tai chi fits equally well into its definition as a sport and an art. So next let us look at the concept of tai chi in the context of fighting and martial arts. My first teacher and her teacher in England denied strenuously my claim that tai chi was in fact a martial art. They defined it only as "a form of moving meditation." Yet the name itself *Tai Chi Quan* means supreme, ultimate fighting art. *Quan* may mean literally fist or form of fighting. It is as much a martial art as nanquan, changquan, shaolinquan or any other variety of *quan*. Whether a teacher decides to teach it as such is an entirely different matter, but its roots in the world of martial arts cannot be denied. The problem lies in the fact that for the most part tai chi is practised slowly, effortlessly and in a tranquil state of mind. But impressions can be deceptive. There is no apparent evidence of aggressive martial spirit and how the movements may be used to deal with an opponent. Only when the tai chi routines are practised as two-person forms or are broken down into their individual constituent techniques, does the martial side become apparent.

In ancient China, tai chi was known as the 13 methods practice. These 13 methods are *Peng* (ward-off) *Lü* (stroke/roll back) *Ji* (press) *An* (push) *Cai* (pull/pluck) *Lie* (twist/split) *Zhou* (elbow) *Kao* (lean with the shoulder) *Jin* (advance) *Tui* (retreat) *Zuo Gu* (glance left) *You Pan* (glance right) *Zhong Ding* (maintain the centre). All of these methods or techniques are present in tai chi routines. Practising the empty hand forms and especially the tai chi weapons forms leads to a greater understanding of the practical applications and effective nature of the 13 methods. Imagining your opponent in front of you as you practise is an excellent means of achieving this aim. However, in order to truly feel and appreciate a deeper understanding, it is necessary to put the self-defence applications to the test by the practice of *Tui Shou* (pushing hands). Pushing hands can teach you a great deal about the soundness of your tai chi forms - whether you are centred, balanced and in alignment and whether you are capable of accurately directing your inner power and energy. It is regrettable therefore that many superior practitioners of tai chi forms are very inadequate at pushing hands. Conversely those who excel in pushing hands are often deficient in their forms practice. I have discovered this phenomenon both in the West and in China. You only have to attend any competition to see two distinct groups of people emerging - those who compete in the forms categories and those who compete in pushing hands. I myself would freely admit that my forms are far superior to my pushing hands ability.

In 1992 I attended the Chinese National Tai Chi and Pushing Hands Championships in Jinzhou. In order to qualify for the pushing hands competition, competitors had first to meet a satisfactory standard in tai chi boxing forms. I have to say that the overall standard was appalling and that I have never witnessed the 42 combination routine being performed so ineptly by so-called tai chi experts in my life. In the pushing hands competition proper, I eagerly awaited a display of subtlety, skill and finesse. However, the contest soon degenerated into bouts of crude grappling and shoving. This was not entirely surprising as many of the participants came from a background not in tai chi chuan but in wrestling. All of this led me to believe that they were not using internal *Jin* energy but hard external force, otherwise known in Chinese as *Li*. This would appear to contradict one of the ten essential points for the practice of tai chi as laid down by Yang Cheng Fu, namely *Yong Yi Bu Yong Li* (用意不用力) - Use the mind, do not use force. *Yi* in Chinese may mean both mind and intention. Real pushing hands as I have observed practised by masters such as Mei Ying Sheng is designed to develop a sensitivity as to the intended movements of your partner. Moreover, it should heighten your awarenesses of your own centre and equilibrium. You should discover not only your partner's weakness but also acknowledge your own weaknesses when your partner finds them. This mutual learning process should enable you to nullify attacks and discover how to turn them to your advantage in the form of counter-attacks. Thus the practice of pushing hands in it purest form as an art serves to demonstrate the functions and practical applications of the thirteen methods of tai chi chuan.

Certain fundamental qualities distinguish tai chi as an art from tai chi as a sport. Tai chi as an art reflects the deeper aspects of traditional Chinese culture. The traditional family style forms handed down from the founder, generation by generation, through the family lineage as a sacred and treasured heirloom represent tai chi as an art. These forms possess a unique family style, spirit and flavour. The modern wushu tai chi forms devised by a group of experts which blend the major styles into a hybrid end-product represent tai chi as a sport. The modern routines are taught in sports schools or Institutes of Physical Culture just like any other sports event. In the Shenyang Institute, you could study basketball, gymnastics, football or any other sport including wushu. It was principally a question of learning a routine to an acceptably high standard for the purpose of presenting an external performance. Traditional tai chi is taught by masters descended from the founder or by disciples and close students of these family heirs. Traditional tai chi is not precluded from being a competitive event. Indeed most international tournaments include specific categories for Yang, Chen, Wu and Sun styles as well as wushu tai chi. It is regrettable to report, however, that the Chinese National Tai Chi Championships only include the modern newly devised forms in the four principal family styles. Many traditional masters feel that these routines do not entirely conform to the requirements of traditional tai chi. At least as a competitive event, judges are instructed to assess traditional tai chi in terms of internal content rather than simply an ability to perform an external routine in slow motion. Traditional tai chi is steeped in culture, whereas wushu tai chi is not.

The best illustration of the difference between traditional and sports tai chi would be to simply look at the names of the movements. Let us take tai chi sword for example. The standard 32 sword form is based on traditional Yang style tai chi sword. In the original form there are certain categories of names concerned with astronomical phenomena, fables, folklore and traditional Chinese festivals. They provide a rich tapestry of beautiful imagery to enhance the aesthetic quality of the movements. Other categories highlight the postures and ways of moving of particular birds or animals. Finally, metapors and idioms are drawn from Chinese literature which enhance the beauty of the movements and lend them a degree of significance. In the modern sword form, all of this is lost. Thus *Liu Xing Gan Yue* (流星赶月) - Shooting Star Catches the Moon becomes *Fan Shen Hui Pi* (反身回劈) - Turn Round To Cut. *Shizi Yao Tou* (狮子摇头) - Lion Shakes Its Head becomes *Suo Shen Xie Dai* (缩身斜带) - Retreat And Carry Sword. And *Feng Sao Mei Hua* (风扫梅花) - Wind Sweeps Away The Plum Blossom becomes *Xuan Shen Ping Mo* (旋身平抹) - Circle Sword Horizontally. In tai chi as a sport, the external appearance is paramount. It is a question of correctly performing techniques such as *Pi* (劈) - Chop, *Dai* (带) - Carry and *Mo* (抹) - Wipe. In traditional tai chi every movement is also heavy with cultural, linguistic and historical significance. That is not to say that the external is unimportant in traditional tai chi. In fact the external form is a reflection of the internal content and harmony. Every movement and posture must be perfect in order to allow the *Qi* energy to flow smoothly around the body.

It could be argued in fact that traditional tai chi is not primarily concerned with movement at all but rather with ideas, concepts, images and beliefs. The form and its intrinsic movements are simply physical manifestations clothing this internal content. It is steeped in the philosophy of Daoism and is merely the physical expression of the concepts of *Yin* and *Yang*. It is the reflection of the *Tai Ji Tu* (太极图) - The tai chi diagram. This is a Daoist symbol depicting the two opposing yet complementary forces of *Yin* and *Yang* which maintain the harmony and equilibrium of the universe - dark and light, soft and hard, yielding and aggressive, feminine and masculine. The *Tai Ji Tu* is often taken to represent tai chi itself. The diagram is made up of two entwined fishes, one black and one white. Each fish is composed of five parts - the head, eye, back, stomach and tail. There is a white eye in the black fish and a black eye in the white fish to show that nothing is wholly *Yin* or *Yang*. The tail of the white fish becomes so narrow that it turns into the head of the black fish and vice versa. This shows that *Yang* taken to its extreme becomes *Yin*, and *Yin* taken to its extreme becomes *Yang*.

Tai Ji Quan itself means supreme ultimate fighting art. The *Ji* or ultimate refers to the extremes of Yin and Yang. Every movement in tai chi is either Yin or Yang. Only at the very beginning and very end of the form when the weight and balance are equally distributed in both feet is one not in a state of *Tai Ji - Yin* or *Yang*. One is rather in a state of *Wu Ji* (无极) - No extreme. In addition to the philosophical content of tai chi, the movements themselves actually mirror the shape of the tai chi diagram. For example, when the arms are raised to shoulder height, the hands palm down, the elbows sunk, and the hands then pushed down beside the hips at the beginning of the form, they describe the outline of the fish on the left hand side of the diagram, from tail (1) to back (2) to head (3) to stomach (4) and back to the tail (1).

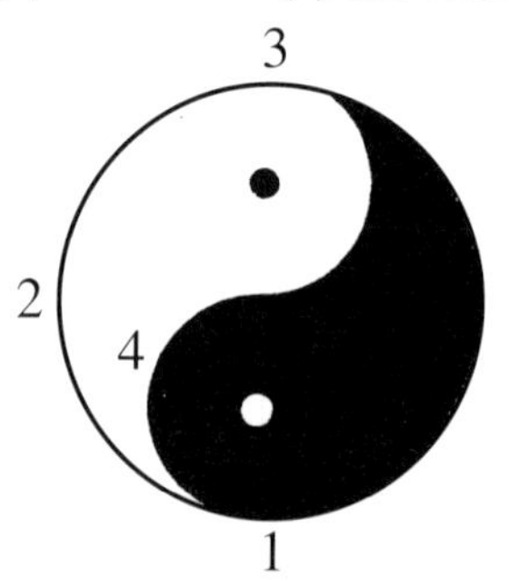

The whole tai chi diagram is contained within a circle. The circle could be seen as representing the earth. It represents the cycle of birth, life and death and the cycle of the changing seasons. It represents the rotation of the earth, the orbit of the planets around the sun and the universe itself. The circle is a symbol of perfection, of progress, of change, of a line without an end. Similarly, the movements of tai chi are circular and the form is practised slowly but in one long, continuous, unbroken line, like drawing a silk thread from a cocoon. Such are the parallels that are drawn between the practice of traditional tai chi and the concepts, ideas and images of Daoist philosophy.

There are many different editions of the simplified 24 forms tai chi chuan routine. The preface to the 1991 edition issued by the Beijing Institute of Physical Education is far more enlightening as to the possible benefits and applications of tai chi than the original published by the China Sports Editorial Board which described tai chi as simply "a means of keeping fit". The motive force for this renewed interest in tai chi lay in the opening ceremony of the Eleventh Asian Games the previous year in Beijing at which fourteen hundred tai chi players from China and Japan gave a mass performance of the 24 step form. This acted as an impetus for many more people to try tai chi themselves. Specifically, this edition put its finger on the medical and health aspects of tai chi. Apart from the obvious benefits of relaxing, toning and strengthening the muscles, medical research has proved tai chi to be instrumental in the regulation of the central nervous system, and the respiratory and cardiovascular systems. It can stimulate intellectual development and inhibit the process of ageing. Not only can it prevent the onset of diseases but also aid and promote the thorough recovery from particular diseases. Notable among these are stress related illnesses, such as high blood pressure and coronary heart diseases.

My master, Mei Ying Sheng, as a retired doctor, surgeon and acupuncturist has carried out a great deal of research in this area based on his own practical experience and real case histories. He is a traditional master with a pragmatic approach. Generally speaking, people nowadays do not want to learn tai chi for its martial applications. Their focus is on relaxation and health promotion. To rigidly adhere to the promotion of tai chi's martial aspects would be to set one's face against the tide of society. Even traditionalists realise that they have to move with the times.

In order to benefit from the healing side of tai chi, it is imperative to explore and harness the internal content. Simply to practise the form will bring the benefits associated with any other aerobic exercise. This is just the surface. The essence of exploring the art of tai chi is the search for the internal. This is what sets it apart from other sports. When I attended the Fiftieth Anniversary Celebrations of the Foundation of the Yongnian Tai Chi Quan Association in Shanghai by Great Grand Master Fu Zhong Wen in 1994, Master Fu in his final address said that he had been engaged in medical research for many years which showed that practising tai chi improved the quality of people's lives. He himself had been the subject of experimentation and the researchers had found that although in his late eighties he still had the body and the constitution of a young man. Traditional masters such as Fu Zhong Wen provide living proof of the benefits of practising tai chi.

However tai chi is regarded, one thing is undeniable, that it is worth preserving as a priceless jewel in Chinese cultural heritage. This is particularly true in the case of tai chi in its traditional form. It is an area of some concern for traditionalist experts and historians. In 1992 Zhang Zhuo Xing wrote an article in the martial arts magazine *Wu Lin* entitled "*Wei Tai Ji Quan Hu Jiu*" (Tai Chi Calling for Help). And in 1993 Professor Zhi Jun wrote an article in *Wushu Jian Shen* entitled "*Chuan Tong Tai Ji Quan Jia Bu Ke Qu Dai*" (Traditional Family Styles of Tai Chi Cannot Be Replaced). The passing on of tai chi chuan is a question of inheritance, handed down from generation to generation. According to the Chinese maxim *Tuo Gui Ju Er Shou Gui Ju* (脱规矩而守规矩) - Cast off old customs yet abide by established practices. We must not stand in the way of progress, believing that the more ancient the better. The integrity of tradition can only be established through tradition's transformation and improvement. The concept of tai chi whether as a sport or an art is constantly evolving.

If tai chi were limited in its definition and practice to only one of its many facets, then its unique appeal, continued growth and rising popularity would be severely restricted. It is tai chi's sheer versatility, very multi-faceted and multi-functional nature which makes it a universal language that transcends the differences between young and old, the sportsman and the artist, the fighter and the philosopher, and crosses international boundaries to join people together in the pursuit of peace and harmony.

How do ordinary people in China view tai chi? In the West we tend to analyse, theorise and mystify tai chi. In China people just do it. We westerners tend to spend a disproportionate amount of time talking about tai chi instead of just going out into the parks and practising it. Talking about tai chi will not produce any beneficial physical, mental and medical effects. However we come to define it - as a sport, a form of moving meditation, a martial art, a medical aid or a traditional art - what is true is that it is a Chinese national treasure worth preserving. The only way that we can be sure of preserving it is if an increasing number of people continue to practise it. So let's just do it.

FLAVOUR : A TASTE OF CHINA

China is a vast country extending from the subtropical province of Guangdong in the south to the plains of Inner Mongolia in the north; from the high plateaux, deserts and mountains of Tibet and Xinjiang in the west to the Yangtze River Delta in the east. This huge diversity in terrain and climate is reflected in the regional cooking styles.

In the bitterly cold, wintry, northern province of Liaoning where I lived for nearly four years the staples are wheat, corn and millet rather than rice, so accounting for the proliferation of dumplings, steamed buns, bread and pancakes. In the south where I lived for a year and a half in the Cantonese city of Shenzhen, rice is the staple and the cooking is much lighter, often using peanut oil rather than the heavy sesame oil favoured in the north. In the western province of Sichuan, the food is renowned for its hot, spicy flavour due to the extensive use of chillies. Rice is more heavily used in the east. Shanghai is well-known for its sweet and savoury dishes.

Food in all its flavours is endowed with the rich symbolism associated with such celebrations as Spring Festival when *Jiaozi* (Dumplings) may be eaten and Mid-Autumn Festival when *Yue Bing* (Mooncakes) are consumed. North, south, east or west, eating plays a central role in the daily life of China and its people. It is closely tied to family life and to traditional rituals.Taste or flavour is an essential element embedded in all aspects of Chinese life.

There is a certain parallel between traditional internal arts and food. In the Chinese culinary art, every item of food may be classified as *Yin* or *Yang*. *Yin* are cool or cold foods. *Yang* are warm or hot foods. A meal should represent the perfect balance of *Yin* and *Yang*, as should a tai chi player's form practice. Generally speaking there are five tastes or flavours which must be present in food : sweet, sour, bitter, pungent and salty. Without each of these flavours being present in the correct proportion, there would be an imbalance. In order to achieve culinary equilibrium, a meal may be divided into two parts according to the concepts of *Fan-Cai*. *Fan* includes staples such as rice, grains, noodles and wheat. *Cai* includes all the other dishes principally made up of vegetables. In the West we often talk glibly about a well-balanced diet. In China this theory is put into practice and is extended to include the concept of a well-balanced life. Food and the practice of internal arts such as tai chi and qigong represent the principal elements of this balanced approach to life.

In China, health is intrinsically tied up with diet. The same food items may be used in medicines as are used in everyday cooking recipes. In Chinese markets, stalls selling spices and medicinal herbs exist side by side. Indeed such is the overlap that restaurants serve dishes specifically beneficial for certain medical complaints. This dual nature of food serves to underline its powers to maintain an equilibrium in the body in terms of health care both mental and physical, as well as in terms of nourishment.

I taught for over a year at the Shenyang Pharmaceutical University where new drugs, both modern and traditional, were being developed. This is one of only two such advanced research establishments in the whole of China, the other being in Nanjing. At the heart of the university was the herb garden which acted as a reminder that even today at the forefront of Chinese medical research and development, traditional ingredients took pride of place. If the garden-keeper allowed me, I would even practise my early morning *Qigong* in the grounds. Later in Shenzhen, my Yang style tai chi master, Mei Ying Sheng, as a retired doctor, was also a nutritionist and would advise me on my diet. It is said that we are what we eat. In China this could not be closer to the truth.

Food as taste; food as tradition; food as ritual; food as a source of balance in life; food as an essential element of good health; food as medicine. Food as a martial art? Food as tai chi even? Well, not quite perhaps. However, they share many of the same elements and there are essential similarities. As we have already seen, Chinese people take the question of taste and flavour very seriously indeed. If a food does not have the required taste, they may say "*Meiyou weir.*" The word in Chinese for taste is *Wei* (味) or *Weidao* (味道). Interestingly enough, *Wei* means both taste and smell, so closely are the two senses related. The *Dao* in *Weidao* is the same *Dao* as in Daoism. One of the major Chinese martial arts competitions in the United States is called "A Taste of China". Even my local Chinese takeaway in London is called "A Taste of China". Food must certainly have taste or flavour. If not, the Chinese tend to add the flavour enhancer known as *Wei Jing* or *Wei Su* which we in the West call monosodium glutamate or MSG. I sometimes heard my tai chi teachers use the expression "*Meiyou Weir*" - (There isn't any flavour) - when referring to someone's practice of tai chi. This set me thinking about what exactly they meant. Obviously, they indicated a lack or deficiency which detracted from the performance. And you couldn't simply add MSG in order to bring the flavour out. Other measures were required. What exactly constituted flavour and how could I go about acquiring it?

In September 1992 I returned briefly to my home in England. This was roughly half way through my course at the Shenyang Institute of Physical Culture. In the previous few months I had attended the Chinese National Wushu Team Championships in Nanchang where I was the only foreigner, the Chinese National Tai Chi And Pushing

Hands Championships in Jinzhou where I was one of only three foreigners and the Chinese National Sports Institutes Championships in Tianjin where I was the only foreigner. There was another foreigner at the Shenyang Sports Institute where I studied. He lived next door to me, but he was Japanese and was studying gymnastics. He spoke no English and I spoke no Japanese so we used to converse in Chinese. My training schedule over the previous six months had been so intense that I was at the peak of my performance. Not only that, but my Chineseness too was very strong. I considered myself half-Chinese and if in public people referred to "the foreigner", it never occurred to me that they were talking about me. Amongst my circle of friends I was known as a "*Zhonguo Tong*" (中国通) which means someone who is very familiar with and sympathetic towards China and her people. It indicates a certain degree of knowledge of the language, culture, history and customs of China. It was effectively a way of showing that a foreigner was becoming Chinese. Huddled in my Chinese army coat and cycling along on my clapped out old Flying Pigeon bicycle, I was often mistaken for a Chinese person and in the half light, without really taking a good look at me, I was often addressed as "*Tongzhi*" (同志) - Comrade. *Tongzhi* literally means someone of like mind or having the same objective - in other words dedicated to socialism and communism. I took the fact that they regarded me as one of them as a compliment.

In a magazine I had seen an advertisement for the United States National Chinese Martial Arts Competition to be held in Orlando, Florida. I managed to scrape together enough American dollars to enter three events : wushu tai chi (42 international competition form), traditional Yang style and internal weapons. So I flew off to the USA for the Labour Day weekend at the beginning of September. I had never entered a competition before in the West but had supreme confidence in my ability (for a man of 40 odd!) and thought that it would be an interesting and revealing experience to pit myself against other tai chi players. I was curious more than anything to see how my standard stood up in comparison. I had no expectations of winning. I was totally unknown in America. What would they make of me? The enigma that I represented was apparent in the first of my events - the 42 step wushu tai chi - where I was awarded marks ranging from 8.9 down to 8.3 by the five judges. It was noticeable that the lowest marks were given by the American judges and the two highest marks by the Chinese and Chinese/American judges. They presumably must have seen something that the others had not seen or had simply missed. I eventually finished seventh with an average score of 8.5. (An honest assessment of my own standard as borne out by competitions in mainland China and Hong Kong would rate me at around 9.0) The post-competition reaction was a revelation. Several judges and fellow competitors came up to me to tell me how much they had enjoyed my performances, and to ask where and with whom I had been training. When I told them that for the past few years

I had been training in mainland China, they smiled in acknowledgement and said that it showed. There was a certain indefinable quality that set me apart from the others, many of whom had also trained with excellent Chinese coaches and masters but in the United States. I wasn't too disappointed not to have won anything but was delighted with the feedback that I was receiving. In the traditional Yang style section I felt that I was actually the only competitor performing Yang style. Some of what passed as Yang style bore not even the slightest resemblance to my understanding of what Yang style should be like. After the competition, the chief judge who had awarded me the highest individual mark told me that in his opinion I was the only competitor performing traditional Yang style correctly and comforted me not to be too downhearted by the result. Another judge told me that my performance was graceful and sensual. Or was that sensuous? Well, that's another story entirely! The other judges were universally unimpressed by the standard in this section and the scores were abysmal across the board. Unfortunately I was tarred with the same brush and my average score fell way below my anticipated level.

Determining what exactly constitutes traditional tai chi is not a problem unique to the West. Even after studying for an entire year with one of the foremost Yang style masters in China, I experienced the same divergence of scores in a competition in mainland China in this category. The chief judge awarded me 9.2 - a mark significantly higher than those given by his fellow judges. After the competition, he came up to me and apologized for the ignorance of the other judges who had awarded higher marks to those competitors who had in fact not been performing traditional tai chi at all but the modern Yang style competition routine which contains certain elements that break traditional conventions. The point was that those judges with a discerning eye had perceived something special in my performances. With regard to the Yang style, it was the subtle skills and techniques associated with a unique, individual family style. With regard to the American competition, it was more a question of the Chinese flavour and spirit of my performance. I myself knew that I possessed a certain quality that the others did not. I could see that what they were doing was technically correct but simply lacked that Chinese flavour of spirit and style. This impression was confirmed at a later date. Those competitors who had scored highly in Orlando in 1992 were brought down to earth when I saw them again two years later taking part in competitions in mainland China where they only received scores of around 8.5 as opposed to the scores of nearly 9 awarded in the United States. It was not that the Chinese judges were more strict but that they were aware of a lack of something in performance. The question that I asked myself was : What was this unique taste or flavour? Could it be learned and acquired by a foreigner or had you to be born with it? I believed and others led me to believe by their comments that I possessed it to a certain degree. The performances of the tai chi players trained outside China were technically sound but rather empty and lacking in spirit and definite style. I concluded that it had to do with the fact that I had been training inside China.

Let us at this stage take a close look at the rules and regulations governing the criteria by which tai chi performances are judged and assessed. According to the Rules for International Wushu Routine Competitions laid down by the International Wushu Federation, out of the possible maximum of ten points "Spirit, pace and style account for two points." In Chinese, the word used for spirit is *Jing Shen* (精神) which also means mind, consciousness and essence, so entailing mental, intellectual and spiritual connotations. The word for style is *Feng Ge* (风格). The individual elements of this word are quite interesting. *Ge* by itself means standard, pattern or style. The character *Feng* by itself actually means wind. China is rich in its wide variety of regional cooking styles. I was reminded of this as the phrase *Feng Wei* (风味) denotes a distinctive regional flavour or aspect of local colour. *Feng Wei Cai* (风味菜) means a distinctive regional dish. This served to confirm that an important aspect of tai chi performance and its assessment by Chinese judges was its essential style and a flavour that you could almost touch, taste and smell.

The International Rules continue "Full two points are given to the competitor who performs with fully concentrated mind , natural facial expression and proper pace." In the original Chinese, the underlined words are <u>*Yi Shi Ji Zhong*</u> (意识集中). *Yi* conveys the meaning of idea and intention. The two characters *Yi Shi* together mean mind in the sense of consciousness, being aware of, and a sense of realization. *Ji Zhong* means to focus or concentrate. This may refer to one's thoughts or efforts. This is the full extent of the requirements according to the English translation. However, a glance at the original Chinese version shows some glaring omissions which are not present in the English text. Notable amonst these is the phrase "*Jing Shen Bao Man*" (精神饱满). We have already seen *Jing Shen* used to mean spirit or mind. There is a third connotation at play here. *Jing Shen Bao Man* is a set, four-character idiom meaning vigorously or energetically. So it is not only a question of exhibiting one's spirit and concentrating one's mind, but also displaying one's vigour and energy. Such a wide divergence of interpretation of the criteria for judging the performance of tai chi routines may not at first sight be evident from the English translation. In fact, there is another whole line of requirements in the original Chinese. *Neirong Chongshi* (内容充实) - Substantial or rich in content; *Jiegou Heli* (结构合理) - Of reasonable structure; and finally *Buju Yunchen* (布局匀称) - Of well-balanced or symmetrical layout. These omissions may be of minor importance but it serves to illustrate the importance of understanding Chinese and the rich flavour of its language which conveys so much in its idioms.

It is not only a question of exhibiting one's spirit and concentrating one's mind but also displaying one's energy and vigour. Although originating from within, energy and vigour are perhaps external qualities which could more easily be recognized. The key quality appears to be the internal content of what is going on in the competitor's mind - his consciousness, his awareness, his intention. I take this to mean that the competitor has to show awareness of his movements and postures in relation to the space surrounding his body. The movements should not be empty but should convey the purpose to which they may be put - in other words the martial applications. During practice, Master Mei advised me that I should imagine my opponent in front of me, so lending practical applications to each movement and posture. Piece by piece, I was beginning to put together the jigsaw of what constituted spirit, style and flavour.

The key quality appeared to be what the competitor was thinking during his performance that set him apart from his fellows. How could this be acquired, assessed and measured? However it could be possible, this fact seemed to provide me with part of the answer to my question. It is often something which is said, seen, learned or experienced at a later date which makes the past click into place. Master Mei Ying Sheng later told me that it was the inner spirit which drives the external form. If the internal spirit is empty, so is the external form. Along the same lines, I noted with interest a report on the Orlando competition in February 1993's issue of "Inside Kung Fu". Quote of the tournament was "It's not the form itself, it's the expression" attributed to Hawkins Cheung. Quote of the tournament final attributed to Dave Cater was "All the guys who know anything about martial arts are Chinese and they can't speak English. All the guys who speak English don't know anything about Chinese martial arts." As I speak both Chinese and English, I feel that I fall somewhere in the middle.

This provided me with another clue as to what constituted the magical, missing, intangible ingredient of flavour or taste. A knowledge of Chinese language and consequently an understanding of the culture are invaluable prerequisites to a deeper grasp of tai chi. I shall deal with this at greater length in a separate chapter. However, suffice it to say for the moment that it was possible for those Chinese masters teaching in the West, even with the aid of interpreters, to be explaining aspects of the art too simplistically or superficially due to their inability to express themselves in English or to their perceived lack of understanding in their western students. I have observed Chinese masters teaching foreign students in broken English or with the help of an interpreter and heard and seen at first hand that their original intentions in Chinese were either misinterpreted into English or simply diluted for western tastes. This is no one's fault and I am not trying to apportion blame. It often stems from a well-meaning intention on both sides to please the other side. Lack of understanding can be an embarrassing and disorientating experience. I should know. When I first arrived in

China, I was a complete novice. Chinese people do not like to be placed in a situation where they may lose face or make foreign friends and guests lose face. So the Chinese teacher may tell the foreign student what he thinks the student wishes to hear, to nod and smile approvingly when he says or does something which appears to reaffirm understanding or approval, whilst in fact the student has got it completely wrong.

To illustrate my point about language, how many tai chi students or teachers for that matter in Britain and America know how to write in Chinese *Peng* (掤), *Lü* (捋), *Ji* (挤) and *An* (按), realizing that all four share the same radical (扌) representing *Shou* (手) - Hand. Something as apparently elementary as this never even crosses the minds of most western tai chi practitioners. In fact, the majority of them still pronounce it as "*Tai Chi*" (a concession made in this very book) instead of the correct form "*Taiji*" or "*Taijiquan*". Due to this incorrect pronunciation, an amazing number of tai chi players still confuse in their own minds the "*Chi*" (*Qi* - 气) of "*Chikung*" (*Qigong* - 气功) with the "*Chi*" (*Ji* - 极) of "*Tai Chi*" (*Taiji* - 太极). *Ji* means ultimate/extreme whilst *Qi* means breath/gas/air. Even those who do know the difference have an incorrect image in their minds if they continue to pronounce it as "*Tai Chi*".

The above serves as a simple illustration as to how unclear the concepts of tai chi are in many tai chi players' minds when they are practising. If the external form is the expression of the internal spirit, it was hardly surprising if many competitors' forms failed to display a clarity of spirit and harmony. Their minds were full of English baggage and garbled Chinese words and expressions. If you were ever to see a display by a truly great Chinese master, you would notice a remarkable, transparent and translucent quality, as if the internal and the external expressions of the form were virtually melting into each other. At this level the clarity is such that the form is the spirit and the spirit is the form.

To this day I still practise writing Chinese characters before I go out to practise my tai chi forms. No teacher in China ever instructed me to do this. It is simply a conclusion I have arrived at to help me focus my mind and to maintain the Chinese flavour of my performance even when I am back home in an English environment. Try writing the characters *Tai Ji Quan* (太极拳) before you go out to practise your form. Consider the individual shapes, the radicals, the fact that the character for "hand" (*Shou* - 手) is hidden inside the character for "fist/fighting art" (*Quan* - 拳) There are many tai chi idioms and maxims in Chinese. Study them. Write them down. Memorize them. Incorporate them into your daily routine of practice. Maybe then you can capture some of the essence or flavour of China in your own backyard.

There are two other inter-related aspects which I feel contribute to the Chinese flavour of tai chi practice. The first is lifestyle and the second is diet which brings me back full circle to the beginning of this discourse.The Chinese way of life is much less stressful than that in the West. This fact is borne out by the general lengthening of life expectancy among Chinese people and a much lower incidence of heart disease and cancers. People rise earlier to take morning exercise in the parks, are highly motivated in a positive attitude towards life and believe that exercise, rest and diet have an important role to play in the quality of life. Early morning exercise stimulates the mental and bodily functions. A sleep after lunch helps to recharge the energy levels. A correct balanced diet keeps the system in harmony.

Having lived in China for long, uninterrupted periods, there were several things that I noticed when I first came back to the West. Firstly, how fat people were and secondly how stressful they all seemed. I asked myself what I missed most about China and I found myself replying - the bicycle. The bicycle actually slows down the time it takes for you to go somewhere, to see someone, to get something done. This fact diminishes the sense of urgency you might feel in a car. In addition, it is a great form of exercise for the legs and stomach. I have never been overweight and always thought that I was in pretty good shape. Over time, I noticed that my body shape was actually changing. I lost around a stone and a half in weight, mainly from my buttocks and thighs. I had always wondered how the Chinese could squat so comfortably for ages at a time when I could not. As I lost all this excess fat, and it has to be said some of my muscle, and my body was pared down to its basic shape, squatting became quite easy. A combination of endless hours of daily practice,cycling and a diet of mainly rice and vegetables (*Fan-Cai*) honed my body down to its Chinese tai chi shape. My fine silk suit seemed to hang more loosely and respond more closely to my movements. My muscles grew softer and my body shape became more well-defined. At the Shenyang Institute of Physical Culture, the other Chinese wushu students would joke with me that my muscles were too *Nen* (嫩) which means tender or delicate like the flesh of a young girl or a succulent chicken. At first I took this as an insult. I later found Master Mei Ying Sheng's muscles to be similarly soft. Then I took the earlier comment as a compliment. Master Mei would often ask people to feel how *Rou Ruan* (柔软) - Soft his muscles were. He also seemed to live in his delicate, almost transparent white silk tai chi suit. It was like a second skin. I could not help thinking of the many silkworms which had spun the silk to make his suit and the analogy with the practise of tai chi which should be uninterrupted, like drawing a silk thread from a cocoon.

Finally, in our continuing search for Chinese flavour, let us examine the question from another angle - that of the writings of the Masters themselves. "The Ten Essential Points of Tai Chi Chuan" were laid down by Yang Cheng Fu and recorded by his disciple Chen Wei Ming in his work "*Tai Ji Quan Shu*" - "The Art of Taijiquan" published in 1925. The eighth point states *Nei Wai Xiang He* (内外相合) - Unity and harmony between the internal and the external. It continues *Shen Wei Zhu Shuai, Shen Wei Qu Shi* (神为主帅，身为驱使) - The spirit acts as the master, the body acts as the messenger. In other words, the spirit is the master and the body is at its command. As you can see, translation and interpretation are difficult and the original symmetry and balance of the Chinese characters and their sounds is inevitably lost. *Shen* means both spirit and mind in Chinese. During practice, the tai chi player should concentrate on the spirit and not the *Qi*. Spirit should be evident in the opening (*Kai* - 开) and the closing (*He* - 合) of the movements and postures which mirrors the opening and closing of the mind and spirit as well. You should not concentrate on guiding the *Qi* around the body. This should be accomplished by the correct practice of the form. Besides, the *Shen*/spirit approach leads you to be outward-looking with eyes wide open, whilst the *Qi* approach leads you to be inward looking with the eyes almost closed. The sixth essential point states *Yong Yi, Bu Yong Li* - (用意不用力) - Use the mind. Do not use force/power. The character *Yi* (意) means both mind and intention. During practice, the advanced tai chi practitioner can direct the *Qi* into the form, so lending it a special quality or flavour. This may be discernible both to the trained and the untrained eye. Within each movement there appear to be many other small and subtle contributing movements - circles within circles. I have often observed this phenomenon when training alongside my teachers. Because the meridians in the body are so open, the *Qi* can flow easily and the master can direct his *Qi* outwards with very little apparent preparation. It is because of this subtle skill that real tai chi masters can push their partners around at will without apparently expending any effort. At the Chinese National Tai Chi and Pushing Hands Championships, I observed a Chinese competitor performing a Chen style routine rather badly and trying to simulate the explosive release of energy - *Fa Jin* (发劲). This display was greeted with hoots of derision and laughter from the knowledgeable audience. It provided a salutary lesson that genuine spirit and flavour cannot be faked. The Tai Chi Classics and the works of the masters are rich in abundant advice as to how we should go about acquiring these qualities by dedication, respect for one's art, sheer hard work and not a little humility along the way. We would be well advised to follow them.

The occasional dose of humility is good for everyone. Anyone who has trained with a tai chi master in China will soon discover this. You reach a point where you think that you are catching up with him as you continue to practise and improve. At this very point, he will do something that rocks you back on your heels, just to let you know that he is at least still one step ahead of you. What you cannot acquire by simply copying is the spirit, essence, flavour or taste of tai chi. This only comes with years of practice in a Chinese cultural environment.

I would often think that I was doing the same as my teachers but they had something extra - some indefinable quality. I couldn't quite put my finger on it. I would stand next to my teachers and copy exactly what they were doing. I would stand in front of the full-length mirrors for hours on end and endlessly practise each movement in minute detail. Still they weren't the same. Maybe it was all done by mirrors. I am still looking.

There is a wide diversity of martial arts styles found in China, each of which has its own distinctive characteristics which may be popularly known as taste or flavour. Southern Chinese martial arts differ greatly from the martial arts of Northern China. Moreover, each traditional style of tai chi is closely associated with one individual family which lends it a particular character. This character is a result of the distillation of the accumulated wisdom of its unique traditional lineage. Finally, each person's performance of tai chi possesses flavour to a greater or lesser extent according to the breadth of his experience, the sheer number of hours of his practice, the external expression of his internal content and his immersion in Chinese tradition, language and culture. The flavour is in the art. The flavour is in the family. The flavour is in the form. And the flavour is in the self.

SOFTNESS WITHIN HARDNESS, HARDNESS WITHIN SOFTNESS

It could be argued that softness within hardness and hardness within softness are the ultimate goals of external styles and internal styles respectively. External stylists firstly train their bodies in hard energy before eventually introducing softness. Conversely, internal stylists strive to develop a physical softness before adding a steely hardness.There is a martial arts saying "*Wai Lian Jin Gu Pi, Nei Lian Yi Kou Qi*" - (外练筋骨皮，内练一口气) - Externally train muscles, bones and skin. Internally train one mouthful of *Qi*. In order to summon up the greatest amount of energy, you need to harness the external manifestations of power as well as the internal expressions of *Qi* energy. Whether you are an internal or an external stylist, you need to concentrate equally on the development of the physical self and the spiritual self. Although the two extremes of external and internal are at first glance apparently working in opposite directions, their ultimate aim is closer than supporters of both camps might believe.

With specific reference to tai chi, it can be practised at several different levels. Some people are happy to be able to practise a tai chi form correctly at a physical level. Others seek contentment in achieving the mental tranquillity that tai chi training can bring. Such physical and mental states can be attained after only a year or two's practice. However, there are much deeper and more complex levels to be attained if one has the time, energy, application and guidance of a master. At the very beginning, the student simply imitates the outer movements one by one and links them together to form a complete routine. Then having learned the principles on which the movements are based, the student tries to put these principles into practice so they are at one with the movements. Finally the principles are combined with the applications to arrive at the essence of tai chi chuan. One layer is laid upon another. In parallel, the student should be sequentially passing through the stages of looseness, softness and finally hardness within softness.

Just what exactly is meant by looseness, softness and hardness? Looseness is a translation of the Chinese character *Song* (松) and is the basic principle in tai chi training. This is the first stage one must achieve. It entails relaxing the body whilst maintaining an essential element of energy or even tension in order to ensure that the movements are held together so as to be performed correctly and coherently, and each fixed posture is strictly adhered to. Softness is the next stage. This is a translation of the Chinese characters *Rou Ruan* (柔软) which separately each means soft or flexible but which are most commonly encountered together as a bisyllable concept. According to Yang Cheng Fu, the sixth essential requirement for the correct practice of tai chi is "*Yong Yi Bu Yong Li*" (用意不用力) - Use the mind, do not use force. Having achieved looseness, one must learn to generate, accumulate and direct *Qi* energy and then use the mind to guide the energy around the body. Softness is to move through the form, filling each movement and posture with elastic internal energy. The final stage is to add hardness, which is a translation of the Chinese character *Gang* (刚), back to the softness. Yang Cheng Fu stated that according to the Treatise on Tai Chi Chuan, "*Ji Rou Ruan, Ran Hou Neng Ji Jian Gang*" (极柔软然后能极坚刚) - From an extreme of softness there comes extreme hardness. Loosenesss and softness in themselves are insufficient. They must be supplemented and complemented with the hardness associated with power.

Let us now examine the different natures of power. There are two distinct types. External power which relies principally on muscle strength is called *Li* (力). It requires that the muscles should be in a state of tension and therefore what is delivered is hard energy. It is possible to possess *Li* without first having passed through looseness and softness. However, internal stylists would argue that this power is as nothing compared with the internal power emanating from softness. This power is called *Jin* (劲) which is a combination of *Li* and *Qi*. It is internal and cannot be seen so much as felt. It is emitted from within and requires that it should be led by the mind. The muscles are relaxed and reinforced with *Qi*, so constituting soft energy. As can be seen from the respective Chinese characters, the symbol for *Li* is contained within the character for *Jin* with the addition of the *Gong* (工) radical. This is also the same radical included in *Qigong* (气功) so implying the addition of a certain special skill. The arms of a tai chi master are said to be *Ru Mian Guo Tie* (如绵裹铁) - Like cotton wrapped around iron. The power is contained and concealed inside, whereas with external arts the power is always superficial and apparent on the outside. It is transient in so far as the power is only in existence when it is summoned up to be discharged. In tai chi, the power is always there in a latent state internally and can be regenerated from without or within, yet is never completely used up. This accounts for the fact that in many of the Tai Chi Classics internal energy is likened to the constant flow and surging power of a river. In Wang Zong Yue's "Thirteen Postures" it states "*Jing Ru Shan Yue, Dong Ru Jiang He*" (静如山岳，动如江河) - Still like lofty mountains, move like a river. In fact, if one examines the old complex character for Jin, there is a further clue to this very effect. *Jin* (勁) shows in the top left hand corner the radical (巛) which represents (川) - *Chuan* meaning river. Internal energy possesses certain qualities not present in external energy and which can be expressed through softness. Softness and hardness are opposites. They are extreme manifestations of the same phenomenon, just as are *Yin* and *Yang*.To reconcile hardness within softness requires a certain skill. What this skill is, where it comes from and how it can be acquired are points which I shall try to address later in this chapter. The fact remains that a mastery of both extremes is essential in order to reach the highest levels of tai chi practice.

It is vitally important not only to understand the principles of tai chi but to put them into effect correctly. Many casual practitioners of tai chi fail even to achieve the first stage of looseness. Most people are either too stiff in their muscles and joints or they are too relaxed, with the result that their forms become shapeless and ill-defined. It is important that the mind as well as the body is calm and relaxed. The tenth essential requirement according to Yang Cheng Fu is "*Dong Zhong Qiu Jing*" (动中求静) - In the midst of movement, seek tranquillity. The movements should be performed as slowly and effortlessly as possible in one continuous stream from the beginning of the form to the end. Just as looseness or relaxation should not equate to loss of shape and physical control, so calm and tranquillity should not equate to a wandering of the focus and concentration of the mind, a lack of awareness and consciousness. True relaxation is a combination of the body, the mind and the internal energy.

The most common word my teachers ever used throughout my training in China was *Song* (松) which means loose or *Fang Song* (放松) which means relax or loosen. The third essential requirement for the correct practice of tai chi as laid down by Yang Cheng Fu is "*Song Yao*" (松腰) - Relax the waist. As the waist acts as the axis, initiation and coordination for all tai chi movements, it is hardly surprising that so much emphasis should be placed on the loosening and relaxation of the waist.

The second most common word used in my training was *Chen* (沉) which means to sink as in the fifth essential requirement expressed by Yang Cheng Fu : "*Chen Jian Zhui Zhou*" (沉肩坠肘) - Sink the shoulders and drop the elbows. The elbows should be kept down in order to keep the shoulders relaxed. Otherwise the shoulders will also be raised and the Qi will rise, so diminishing the intrinsic power in the body. This is also closely related to the second essential requirement "*Han Xiong Ba Bei*" (含胸拔背) - Round the chest and raise the back. This particular principle engages the loosening of the waist which enables it to direct the energy. Sinking the shoulders, dropping the elbows, hollowing the chest and rounding and raising the back all contribute to the generation of energy. Staying loose in the waist and hips does not simply mean the ability to turn the body on an axis, but to free the legs, the thorax, the shoulders and the arms so that all the parts of the body act in concert and in a coordinated fashion. By working hard at staying loose and relaxed, by concentrating on sinking and dropping in the shoulders and arms, by pulling up through the back and down through the hips and waist, the body will not only become loose but also soft , so developing natural, internal energy without actually trying. What is more, the body will become firmly rooted. Amateur practitioners of tai chi do not always understand or appreciate principles such as these, so how can they hope to graduate to the higher levels? Others know the principles but this is not the same as putting the principles into practice. Others again think of looseness or softness as an end and achievement in itself and their movements become loose or soft to the point of weakness where the dynamic connection between the parts of the body has been overextended with the result that the individual movements are no longer part of a whole. Correct understanding, interpretation and practice of the concepts of *Song* and *Chen* are essential.

Softness does not only mean looseness or suppleness. At the Shenyang Sports Institute I observed international class athletes training at close quarters on a daily basis. In the same building and one floor above the *Wushu* training hall, was the gymnastics centre. Gymnasts and particularly rhythmic gymnasts possessed extremely supple bodies which enabled them to perform the most intricate physical feats, but I could not describe their bodies as displaying the same qualities of softness that I witnessed in my tai chi coaches. Their bodies were certainly stretched to the limits and their movements were fluent and graceful but there was still a certain element missing. To the touch their muscles were toned and hard, unlike mine which, although equally strong, were very soft and pliable. The Chinese students described my muscles as *Nen* (嫩) which means tender or delicate like the flesh of a young girl or the meat of a succulent chicken. In order to attain softness, Mei Ying Sheng emphasized the isolation of every joint in every movement. When curving back the arm, for example, the loose extension of the limb should be felt from the shoulder right down to the finger joints and tips. This process is aided by the concentration of the *Yi* - the mind. It is as if all the joints of the body are threaded together on a string. Master Mei Ying Sheng's muscles were also described as *Nen* and extremely *Rouruan* (柔软) - Soft but still immensely strong. It was this softness and strength that I set out to achieve.

The practice of tai chi represents and expresses the idea of unity of flow. This is a chief characteristic of an internal style. "*Yun Jin Ru Chou Si*" (运劲如抽丝) - Transport the energy as if drawing silk is a concept referred to in the Tai Chi Classics and echoed in Yang Cheng Fu's Ten Essential Requirements. The ninth point states "*Xiang Lian Bu Duan*" (相连不断) - Linked together without breaking, in other words, continuity without interruption. This is an obvious source of the development of softness. The whole tai chi routine is one complete, continuous, uninterrupted movement made up of circles and circles within circles. This is what is referred to in the Tai Chi Classics as "*Ru Chang Jiang Da He, Tao Tao Bu Jue*" (如长江大河，滔滔不绝) - Like a big long river, surging like a torrent without ceasing. This is in contrast to external styles where the flow of movements may be broken, intermittent and performed with tension and the deliberate use of power. Each burst of power is used up before a new one is generated, whereas in tai chi there is one long, continuous surge of energy travelling unhindered throughout the form like a fine strand of silk being drawn from a cocoon. Those who practise tai chi with a deliberate, mechanical or jerky form of movement will never be able to develop softness nor generate internal power as they are guilty of *Duan Jin* (断劲) - Breaking the energy flow. The internal river of *Qi* circulation reflects, complements and drives on the external river which flows in one continual movement.

When practising tai chi and moving from one posture to another, when changing from a state of *Yin* to a state of *Yang* and vice versa, there should be a definite *Kai* (开) - Opening and *He* (合) - Closing of the body. This will effectively loosen and stretch out the muscles, open the meridians, stimulate the circulation of blood and *Qi* and gradually make the body stronger and stronger. Most people who practise tai chi inefficiently do not successfully complete the functions of *Kai* and *He* and no physical benefits are derived. In fact each movement in tai chi should be composed of four parts : *Qi, Cheng, Zhuan, He* (起承转合) - Rising/Opening, Carrying, Turning and Closing. Each component part is complementary to and of mutual service to the others. Opening, carrying and turning serve to bring about closing. The first three elements are the means and closing is the end. If the opening is incorrect or incomplete, the succeeding elements cannot be successfully completed. As most people who practise tai chi do not complete the opening phase, the other three phases are either very weak or non-existent. The form exists in a twilight world between Opening and Closing, between *Yin* and *Yang*, where extremes are never touched. Consequently little or no progress is made, no matter how much one may practise. The meridians are never fully opened and the Qi does not flow unhindered. The levels of looseness and softness can never be attained.

Tai chi comprises thirteen postures including eight basic energies : *Peng* (掤), *Lü* (捋), *Ji* (挤), *An* (按), *Cai* (采), *Lie* (挒), *Zhou* (肘) and *Kao* (靠). Ward off, roll-back, press, push, pluck, split, elbow strike and lean with the shoulder. Whilst each of these energies has its own characteristics, they are inter-related. And *Peng* ward-off energy is at the heart of every movement and every posture. Different tai chi styles place different emphasis on different energies. Yang style emphasizes *Peng Jin* (掤劲) whereas Chen style places greater emphasis on *Chan Si Jin* (缠丝劲) - Reeling silk energy, in view of the spiralling movements particular to its style. According to Wang Zong Yue in his Intellectual Interpretation of the Thirteen Postures, "*Xu Jin Ru Zhang Gong, Fa Jin Ru Fang Jian*" (蓄劲如张弓，发劲如放箭) - Storing up the *Jin* is like drawing back the bow, Letting out the *Jin* is like releasing the arrow. This release of explosive energy is called *Fa Jin* (发劲) and is most evident in Chen style tai chi. One could say it was the external manifestation of hardness within softness. The sudden release of energy should nevertheless be accompanied by the muscles remaining relaxed and loose rather than tense and tight. It is not an abrupt impulse of energy discernible in the movements of the tai chi practitioner himself. The *Yi* (mind/intention) leads, followed by the the *Jin* and enhanced and empowered by the *Qi*. In a martial respect, all of the above energies have to be mastered and are particularly relevant in the practice of pushing hands, as well as placing every fixed posture in a martial context from the point of view of its practical application.

Pushing hands practice requires particular skills with regard to *Jin*. Firstly, you need to be able to *Dong Jin* (懂劲) - Understand *Jin*, then to grasp the intention of your opponent by the process of *Ting Jin* (听劲) - Listening to the *Jin* which entails becoming sensitive to his strengths and weaknesses so that the energy can be neutralized and turned back round against him. This skill is accomplished by developing a kind of intuition or other sense. When you are sticking or adhering to your opponent, the ability to listen is paramount. The deeper meaning of listening to your opponent is not immediately apparent to the westerner. The modern simplified Chinese character *Ting* (听) for listen is made up of two radicals : *Kou* (口) meaning mouth and *Jin* (斤) meaning axe, which does not tell us a great deal. However, the old complex Chinese character for *Ting* (聽) is made up of *Er* (耳) - the ear, *Mu* (目) - the eye, and *Xin* (心) - the heart. This indicates much more clearly the senses and sensitivities which should be utilized in pushing hands. You have to listen, to watch and to feel. When performing the empty hand routines, you have to imagine your opponent in front of you and visualize how each movement and fixed posture might be used in a martial context. However, deprived of physical contact, you cannot be sure how strong your ward-off energy or reeling-silk energy are, nor whether they would be genuinely effective in a free-fighting situation. The advantage of pushing hands is that by sticking to your opponent you are able to use a wide range of energies in a practical way against a physical presence whilst still testing your own powers of coordination, rooting, looseness and softness.

There is still another vital area of tai chi training that I have not yet touched upon which is essential for reaching the final phase of hardness within softness. This is the area of weapons and power training. Power training would be anathema to many internal stylists. This blinkered approach, however, precludes them from reaching the highest levels of tai chi practice - hardness within softness. I would contend that part of the secret to attaining this level lies in the domain of tai chi weapons. Tai chi practitioners from a non-martial background have an aversion to weapons such as sword and broadsword which in their eyes have no place in tai chi training. It is for this very reason that the field of tai chi weapons has been neglected in an era and an environment where tai chi is primarily studied for health and meditation. Few teachers in the West have a competent grasp of even basic sword techniques, let alone broadsword, staff , spear or other more esoteric weapons. However, the truth is that they form a vital and integral part of the tai chi repertoire.

Once *Qi* has been generated internally, the next step is to develop the skill of externalizing this energy. The sword for example is simply an extension of the hand and the arm. Using the mind to direct the *Qi* outside the body into the weapon and focusing on the tip or other striking area of the blade requires a higher degree of skill than internal energy circulation. Modern tai chi swordplay is performed with a loose, non-descript grip, and contact with the handle is often limited to the thumb and index finger. Traditional swordplay as described elsewhere in this book has a wide variety of grips and possesses qualities of both *Yin* and *Yang*. There are in excess of twenty different sword techniques, all of which are subtly different and require that the energy be directed to a specific point of the blade, using the tip and both striking edges. Broadsword, or sabre as a single-edged weapon, involves completely different techniques from the sword and is another rich source for the development of energy. However, the area of weapons training from which power can really be generated is the spear. Interestingly enough, during my tai chi training at the Shenyang Sports Institute, I dabbled in a little staff and spear. But to show the members of the wushu team that I was more than just a geriatric practising internal styles such as tai chi and bagua, I decided to take up the *Da Dao* (大刀) - Halberd which was the heaviest weapon in the wushu armoury. Although lending it a certain tai chi flavour, to the amazement of my fellow students, I found that I was able to wield the Halberd swiftly, fluently, and what was even more significant, powerfully throughout the routine. Not only that, once I returned to my tai chi forms, I discovered that my movements had been reenergized. I was therefore not surprised to discover that Guan Tie Yun, my chief coach at the Institute, was the 1973 Liaoning Province spear champion among his many other achievements in internal arts. It became evident that training with weapons required certain skills and particular energies which added significantly to the quality and depth of tai chi training.

Spear is a particular case in point. It is acknowledged as the most demanding of weapons, necessitating great strength and control. The one technique particular to the *Qiang* (枪) or spear is *Dou* (抖) - Shaking, which requires the entire length of the spear shaft as well as the tip to vibrate with energy. *Dou Gan* (抖杆) - Shaking the shaft/pole of the spear can increase the inner energy of both arms so that they are not only strong but also pliable. The particular Chinese character to describe this quality is *Ren* (韧) which interestingly contains the radical *Dao* (刀) meaning knife, as well as the character *Ren* (刃) meaning edge of the blade of a sword which of course has to be both pliable and strong. It is said that the technique of thrusting out the spear *Chu Qiang* (出枪) should be performed thus : "*Rou Zhong Yu Gang*" (柔中寓刚) - In the midst of softness resides hardness and that the artist should be "*Song Rou Chen Wen*" (松柔沉稳) - Relaxed, soft, calm and stable so that the internal energy can reach the tip of the spear. In traditional tai chi spearplay there also exists a two-person form called *Si Nian Qiang* (四粘枪) which literally means four sticky spear. It was thus called because of the four vital areas of a person's body which were open to attack by the spear : feet, shoulders, neck and heart. In the practice of *Si Nian Qiang*, the object is to literally stick to your opponent at all times using *Zhanlian* (沾连) - adhering. According to the book "*Tai Chi Chuan Shu*" by Gu Liu Xin, this sticky spear practice evolved out of the *Ting Jin* method of internal sensitivity in pushing hands. The above parallels and this revelation bring us full circle from the softness acquired through forms practice to the addition of a certain whip-like resilience in pushing hands to the subtle externalization of energy in sword play to the steely hardness of long weapons such as halberd and spear.

Despite the weight of arguments, some people still find it hard to reconcile the concepts of softness and hardness within softness in the field of tai chi. They consider that tai chi is an internal style and therefore inherently soft. However, they lose sight of the fact that tai chi, amongst its many other facets, is a martial art and that its movements have purpose and practical applications. In China it is quite normal for youngsters to train in *changquan, nanchuan* or other forms of external arts from the age of five or six. As they mature, they take up internal styles such as *tai chi, xingyi* or *bagua*. This is a natural progression. They thus possess a much more broadly based and rounded education in martial arts. In the West, most people come to tai chi at a mature age from a non-martial background. They have a natural aversion to external fighting or martial arts per se and prefer to dwell on the internal, meditational and healing aspects of tai chi. They fail to grasp the inherent and implicit connection between the internal and the external. Yang Cheng Fu's eighth essential requirement states "*Nei Wai Xiang He*" (内外相合) -Internal and external combine together. There should be unity and harmony between the internal and the external. It is said that the spirit is the master and the body is at its command. There is a martial arts saying "*Lian Quan Bu Lian Gong, Dao Lao Yi Chang Kong*" (练拳不练功，到老一场空) - If you train in *Quan* and not in *Gong*, when you get old, all that is left is emptiness. This means that if you only dwell on the externals of the form and neglect the development of the internal energy, in the end you will have nothing. Another saying along similar lines goes "*Hua Quan Xiu Tui*" (花拳绣腿) meaning flower fist and embroidered leg, implying that a martial artist who practises without internal substance is guilty of presenting something which is aesthetically pleasing but totally devoid of content. Techniques by themselves are empty if there is nothing on the inside. As you get older and your physical strength deteriorates, if there is no complementary internal strength, then you will be left with nothing. There is thus a strong argument for developing both internal and external energies.

Whatever stage the tai chi exponent has arrived at in his development - looseness, softness, or hardness within softness - he must never lose sight of the basic principles of tai chi and always try to put them into practice. There should be a balance of *Yin* and *Yang* within the body and the mind. Looseness simply means relaxing your entire body whilst still retaining enough energy for the movements and postures of the tai chi routine to be held together under a certain thread-like tension, so connecting the parts to the whole. Softness is to move within looseness using the mind or intent to guide the internal energy with each joint open, stretched and isolated. There is relaxation, concentration and calmness of the mind. The tenth and final essential requirement according to Yang Cheng Fu is "*Dong Zhong Qiu Jing*" (动中求静) - In the midst of movement, seek calm. The *Qi* should initially sink to the *Dan Tian*. By practising tai chi slowly, effortlessly, continuously and easily over a prolonged period, accompanied by deep, slow, abdominal breathing, you will achieve an extraordinarily powerful source of internal energy. If you are patient. Correct practice in this manner will allow the *Qi* to sink deeply to the *Dan Tian* from which it may be circulated throughout the entire body, even permeating and penetrating the muscles and bones. The internal energy can be collected, circulated, distributed and if necessary transmitted for either healing or martial purposes. Meanwhile, the head should be light and suspended as if by a thread. The vital energy should rise from the upper *Dan Tian* known as the *Yin Tang* (印堂) midway between the eyebrows to the point at the crown of the head called in acupuncture the *Bai Hui* (百会), which is at the uppermost point of the *Du* Meridian, the controlling channel. At this stage your mind will be perfectly clear and calm. There will be a balance of *Yin* and *Yang* within the mind as well as the body. From this point, what is important is the correct practice of the tai chi form. It is said that the external form leads the internal *Qi*. And the internal *Qi* drives the external form. These functions are complementary. Ideally, the same form should be practised five or six times in a row, paying equal attention to the external and the internal. In this way, a balanced approach should yield genuine progress and access to the higher levels of the art.

At times during my five years in China I wondered despairingly if I could ever approach the standards set by my teachers. Occasionally I felt that I was getting close, only for them to to do something which elevated them to a completely different plane. Over time I realized that this catching up process was all part of my apprenticeship. I had to pass through different stages of development at both a mental and physical level. Whilst these two strands of my tai chi education took place independently to a certain extent, I was aware that these two parallel lines were gradually coming closer, eventually to meet each other at the horizon. I read the Tai Chi Classics, studied the principles, listened to the arguments and wisdom of my teachers, And I put this accumulated knowledge into practice in my tai chi. I practised and I practised and I practised as in the Chinese saying "*Shu Neng Sheng Qiao*" (熟能生巧) - Practice makes perfect. Slowly, imperceptibly at first, without consciously trying to catch up and match my teachers, I realized that I was improving, progressing, growing through the sheer weight of practice and hard work. When I look back now, I can perceive the different phases that I passed through - firstly achieving looseness, then softness and finally hardness within softness. I feel that I have only just entered the final phase. Perhaps with another 25 years of practice I may achieve proximity to my teachers. "Bu Dao Huang He, Xin Bu Si" (不到黄河心不死) - Don't give up hope until you reach the Yellow River.

It appears futile to me to argue about the relative merits of which power is the greater - the internal or the external. Whether *Jin* (劲) internal energy is more potent than *Li* (力) external power. As we have already seen from the Chinese characters, the symbol for *Li* is contained within that for *Jin* with the additional radical of *Gong* (工). Perhaps they are not two separate entities after all but inextricably bound together. According to the Tai Chi Classics, the intent should lead the internal energy and the internal energy should lead the power. When the intent arrives, the internal energy arrives and when the internal energy arrives, the power arrives. People are deluded into believing that only external stylists are strong because they develop big muscles and train hard whereas internal stylists train very little and conjure up their power from the thin air by contemplating and meditating for inordinately long periods. It is all too easy to think that masters of internal arts in their seventies, eighties or even their nineties are doddering, frail, old gentlemen with benign smiles who rely solely on their internal energy or the willing complicity of their docile disciples to push their young students around. In fact, these are people who have trained up to as much as ten hours a day since their youth and who were also quite possibly champions in external styles at about the age of twenty before they graduated to internal styles. The truth is that Masters of both internal and external disciplines are both immensely strong in a physical sense. Any student who has worked with one on a day to day basis over a period of time will testify to this.They have both developed tremendous rooting powers, superb coordination and execution of techniques. They are thus not so far apart as some would lead us to believe. If one accepts that tai chi is equally an art for generating *Qi* for the benefits of mental and physical health and at the same time a martial art for self-defence, then these two elements can co-exist comfortably in parallel and even complement each other without any contradiction.

To achieve softness and even hardness within softness requires many hours of relentless, dedicated and correct practice under the supervision and guidance of a master. It may be unrealistic and impractical to expect such dedication nowadays. But if one doesn't set targets, one will never achieve anything.This is echoed in the Chinese maxim "*You Zhi Zhe Shi Jing Cheng*" (有志者事竟成) However, it is important to persevere and keep trying even if at first the rewards for one's efforts may seem small. "*Bing Dong San Chi, Fei Yi Ri Zhi Han*" (冰冻三尺， 非一日之寒) - Three feet of frozen ice is not the result of one day's cold weather.

LANGUAGE AS THE KEY TO CULTURE

The Chinese word for contradiction is *Maodun* (矛盾) which is made up of the two characters for spear (矛) and shield (盾). By a typical Chinese contradiction or paradox, this chapter could equally well have been titled "Culture as the key to language", so closely are the two inextricably inter-related. *Maodun* usually describes some kind of conflict at work within one's pattern of speech or behaviour. It forms part of a four-character idiom, *Zi Xiang Mao Dun* (自相矛盾) which means to be self-contradictory. But why spear and why shield? The explanation is as follows. The writer, Han Fei Zi (韩非子) in his article "*Nan Shi*" (难势) - A Difficult Situation, described a merchant selling both spears and shields. When he described the hardness of his shields, he was insistent that nothing could penetrate them. And when he praised the sharpness of his spears, he insisted that there was nothing that they could not pierce. Someone who perceived the contradiction inherent in his two conflicting statements asked the merchant, "What would happen if you used your spear against your shield?" The merchant could not reply.

Sayings, idioms and maxims form an integral part of everyday Chinese. They are rooted in folklore, myths and legends, traditional festivals and classical literature. A knowledge of the Chinese language is evidently a key to the understanding and appreciation of the above manifestations of culture in their original form. Likewise a knowledge of Chinese culture will facilitate a greater comprehension of the language itself.

Chinese is the oldest living language. China and its people have experienced the longest span of cultural development of any society in the world. Chinese culture and tradition are therefore particularly deep-rooted. The influence of China's long cultural past is present in the language, the folklore, government and business practices, the social environment, interpersonal relations and of course martial arts.

The national language of the People's Republic of China is *Putonghua* which means the common language and is based on the Beijing dialect. A good dictionary will include more than 10,000 characters. There are about five and a half to six thousand characters in active and passive everyday use. Knowledge of about three and a half thousand characters should enable you to read and understand 99% of the contents of a Chinese newspaper. In mainland China, complex characters have been simplified so that they contain fewer strokes and are therefore easier to identify and learn. By way of example, the complex Chinese character for dragon - *Long* (龍) containing sixteen strokes has been reduced to (龙) containing just five strokes. The Chinese character for China itself is of interest in this respect. The modern simplified form of China is *Zhong Guo* (中国) - The Central Country. The character Guo meaning country comprises the jade radical *Yu* (玉) representing the Emperor within an outer boundary. The old complex form for *Guo* (國) is a combination of the mouth radical *Kou* (口) representing the people, and the weapon radical *Ge* (戈) meaning an ancient dagger or axe, so representing defence within the boundary of the country.

Several different systems have been devised for transcribing Chinese characters into romanized script. The most widely used and officially endorsed system is called *Pinyin*. Every effort has been made to simplify the language in order to aid effective learning and to make it more accessible. Similarly in the field of martial arts, tai chi has been simplified for the very same reasons. The simplified 24 forms tai chi chuan was devised in 1956 by the Chinese State Commission for Physical Culture and Sports in order to promote and popularise a simplified form of an ancient traditional art. Unfortunately, simplification and accessibility do not necessarily go hand in hand with understanding. This is true, whether it is applied to language or to tai chi. The language divorced from its culture is almost meaningless. Tai chi distanced from its cultural base is only comprehensible up to a certain point. Language is an intrinsic part of the history of a civilisation. Each civilisation with its culture and language, has its own characteristics which are accepted and tacitly and implicitly understood by its people. These may be difficult to explain for the native Chinese language speakers and even more difficult for a foreigner to grasp. Language is a product of the civilisation and has to be learned and appreciated in that context in order to be fully understood.

The culture of China encompasses many diverse philosophies including Daoism, Buddhism and Confucianism. By culture I mean knowledge, traditional customs and established practices, personal and social values, and a certain code of behaviour. These sets of ideas may be handed down from generation to generation. Confucianism forms the basis of China's cultural tradition with stress being laid on the importance of correct interpersonal relationships. It advocates adherence to old customs and rituals, by looking to the past for role models. The family is the key unit in the social hierarchy so ensuring stability and order. Age is respected in a predominantly patriarchal system. Orientation is towards groups in which the elders and betters are allocated the highest status and authority. All these tenets find a resonance in tai chi and in traditional family style tai chi in particular. The family structure, hierarchy, status, authority and the adherence to traditional customs are aspects common to both. And finally there is the concept of developing one's moral potential within the group framework by fulfilling one's social obligations to one's superiors or masters. It can clearly be seen that there are implicit parallels between Confucianism and the philosophy applied to the practice and transmission of tai chi as an art. Daoism on the other hand is concerned with promoting harmony with the forces of nature. The first lines of Chapter One of the "*Dao De Jing*" by Lao Zi are: "The way that can be told is not the constant way. The name that can be named is not the constant name." In other words, there is no name that can be applied to the Dao because language is an inadequate medium for such a purpose. The question is : What means can be used to convey its entity? Contradictions and opposites add up to a whole. Such contradictory concepts are also to be found in the "*Yi Jing*", the Book of Changes which is one of the five Confucian Classics. By balancing these forces known as Yin and Yang, harmony is achieved in the universe. Tai chi is a language and means of communication in itself. By the constant shifting from a state of Yin to a state of Yang in the form, it is possible to achieve a harmony that is beyond words.

The language barrier is a serious obstacle to learning Chinese martial arts on several levels. At a basic level it prevents the student from communicating with his teacher and so establishing a fundamental rapport. If you do not even have a grasp of the basic commands, responses, names of movements, kinds of stances and hand forms then your training is not even likely to get off the ground. At an intermediate level you need to grasp more complex phrases, be able to question, give and take opinions as well as being familiar with a higher technical vocabulary associated with the correct practice of more advanced techniques. Finally with a master you need to appreciate subtle expressions and nuances of meaning, references to Chinese maxims and idioms, allusions to literature, myths and legends, and have a specialised vocabulary of anatomy and acupuncture. Much is made of Chinese masters being unwilling to give up their ultimate secrets. It is equally possible that the students were unable to receive these secrets due to their linguistic inadequacies. It is all too easy to hide behind language problems.

In the very beginning when I first went to China, the fact that I was a tai chi practitioner and even a tai chi teacher opened many doors to me. This was because I understood and shared their passion for a traditional martial art. Tai chi was a language and a means of communication in itself. It brought me onto the same wavelength as my Chinese counterparts. That was fine up to the point where we were able to share a common experience, with which we were both familiar. However, the process of learning a new form with a new teacher made altogether different linguistic demands.

My inability to speak and understand Chinese was a barrier to the deeper knowledge that any teacher might wish to impart to me. The most common phrases my first teacher used were "*Zai lai yi ci*" - Do it again, "*Cong tou kai shi*" - Start from the beginning and "*Zai lian yi bian*" - Practise it once more. Exercising, repeating and practising are of no use whatsoever if what you are doing is wrong and goes uncorrected. The fault lay entirely with me. At least I acknowledged this shortcoming and took steps to put it right in both the short and the long term, firstly arranging for the services of an interpreter to be present at my classes and secondly engaging a Chinese teacher and knuckling down to learning how to speak, read and write Chinese. I stress all these skills because whilst I needed an oral ability to converse with my teacher, I also needed to be able to read books and write my own notes in Chinese. The services of a friendly interpreter may seem a particularly attractive option to a student learning from a Chinese teacher in the West or in China. However, there are many potential pitfalls. The interpreter may not be a martial arts enthusiast familiar with the specialised and particular terminology. With the best will and intention in the world, even a proficient interpreter may simplify, mislead, misinterpret or merely tell you what he thinks you want to hear or what he thinks was originally in the teacher's mind. Smiles allround. Everyone is satisfied. Everyone apparently understands but the seeds of misunderstanding have been sown. There is ultimately no alternative. You have to learn Chinese.

The question is where do you start? Start with the parts of the body and the names of movements of the form that you are learning. Learn to ask basic questions such as "*Zenmeyang*?" - How is it? "*Hao bu hao*?" - Is it good? "*Dui bu dui*?" - Is it correct? It may be elementary but at least it will elicit a response and engage a dialogue. If you don't understand, say so. "*Wo bu dong*" - I don't understand. "*Zai shuo yi bian*" - Say it again or "*Man dian*" - More slowly. Don't let the teacher think that you know more than you really do or he will end up talking completely over your head. Take it one step at a time. Try to make steady and continual progress. By constant use of the phrases you will soon find that you can get by quite adequately with a limited stock of words and phrases. At least for the time being.

The higher the level of your teacher, coach or master, the greater are the demands made on your language ability and skills and equally your appreciation of Chinese culture. A teacher may be instructing you in simplified or standardized forms. A coach may be training you in competition routines. A master may be teaching you traditional forms. At each step the linguistic level is higher. At the Sports Institute my coaches used a more technical vocabulary involving body mechanics, methodology and precise techniques. Some of them made reference to wushu idioms and even quoted from the Tai Chi Classics to illustrate a point. When learning the competition Chen style form I had the ultimate satisfaction of asking my non-tai chi acquaintances what the character *Dui* (碓) meant. Without fail, none of them knew what it was, but I did. It comes from the movement called Buddha's Warrior Attendant Pounds Mortar - *Jin Gang Dao Dui* (金刚捣碓), an obscure name in itself. Apparently *Dui* means a tilt-operated treadle hammer for threshing rice. No wonder nobody outside the tai chi world knew what it meant! But it gave me as a foreigner a certain kick to be picking up Chinese characters of both the usual and the unusual kind.

It will not have escaped your attention that many of the names of the movements in tai chi forms relate to animals, birds, reptiles and mythical or literary characters. How many students, let alone teachers, know what they mean. Even in the 24 forms simplified tai chi routine where you would expect everything to be simple and straightforward, the names are still complex and rooted in the cultural tradition. Parting the Wild Horse's Mane, White Crane Spreads its Wings, Snakes Creeps Down and Jade Maiden Works at her Shuttles are just a few examples. Traditional tai chi provides us with an even richer cultural tapestry of names. Take the Yang style tai sword form for example. It contains allusions to astronomical phenomena such as *Da Kui Xing* (大魁星) - The Big Dipper and *San Huan Tao Yue* (三环套月) - Three Rings Cover The Moon. Fables such as *Ne Zha Tan Hai* (哪吒探海) - Ne Zha Gauges the Depth of the Sea. Ne Zha was a mischievous little boy who was born inside a ball. He is a character who appears in one of the most famous classical Chinese novels "*Xi You Ji*" (西游记) - The Journey to the West. And *Bai Hu Jiao Wei* (白虎搅尾) - White Tiger Shakes Its Tail. This is an allusion to a Chinese novel called "*Shui Hu*" (水浒) - The Water Margin in which the character Wu Song is fighting with an old white tiger when the fierce creature raises its tail to beat him. Folklore such as the many references to dragons: *Wu Long Bai Wei* (乌龙摆尾) - Black Dragon Waves Its Tail, *Huang Long Chu Shui* (黄龙出水) - Yellow Dragon Emerges from the Water and *Qing Long Xian Zhua* (青龙现爪) - Green Dragon Shows Its Claws. According to legend, the dragon was the king of the water creatures. People in olden times likened the wielding of a sword to a swimming dragon. Hence the origin of the idiom *Jian Ru You Long* (剑如游龙) - Sword Like a Swimming Dragon. Metaphors drawn from literature such as *Da Peng Zhan Chi* (大鹏展翅) - Big Roc Spreads its Wings. The name of this movement is derived from a fable by Zhuang Zi in which an enormous fish called *Kun* is transformed into a bird. Various animal movements such as *Yanzi Chao Shui* (燕子抄水) - Swallow Skims the Water in which the swallow's wing corresponds to the bottom edge of the sword's blade and *Huang Feng Ru Dong* (黄蜂入洞) - Yellow Bee Enters the Nest in which the bee circling around before finally entering its nest is like the movement of the tip of the sword. All the above examples through the richness of the imagery serve to highlight and enhance the aesthetic quality of the sword techniques. Whether it is the modern wushu tai chi or traditional family style tai chi, the cultural heritage shines through in the vocabulary and the quality of the language.

To illustrate to what extent language is deeply embedded in the culture, let me return once more to the theme of dragons. As already observed in the Yang style tai chi sword form, there are several allusions to dragons. In Chen style tai chi also there are movements called *Qing Long Chu Shui* (青龙出水) - Green Dragon Emerges From the Water and *Huang Long San Jiao Shui* (黄龙三搅水) - Yellow Dragon Stirs the Water Three Times. Why this apparent obsession with dragons? Well, the Chinese people actually sometimes refer to themselves as *Long De Chuan Ren* (龙的传人) - Descendants of the Dragon. Emperors of every dynasty have claimed to be *Zhen Long* (真龙) - The Real Dragon. In the Qing dynasty the Chinese flag even bore the dragon as the stamp of imperial authority. In Chinese works of philosophy such as the *Yi Jing*, the dragon is symbolic of a great man. In *Feng Shui*, the energy forces acting upon the fate of mankind are called Dragon Lines. These few examples serve to show the place that the symbol of the dragon occupies in Chinese culture. On the fifth day of the fifth month according to the lunar calendar, the Dragon Boat Festival takes place. The dragon is seen as possessing life-giving powers through the medium of water. It can thus be seen quite clearly that the dragon plays an important role in Chinese traditions, culture and language.

In addition to its literary and cultural tradition, China has a strong oral tradition. Myths evolved out of observations of natural phenomena that appeared to be beyond the scope of human possibility and accomplishment. Legends arose out of social phenomena and historical events. Myths and legends were constantly revised and embellished as they were handed on by word of mouth until they eventually found their way into Chinese folktales. Tai chi also has a strong oral tradition of handing down skills. This may be partly due to the fact that certain masters were illiterate or simply to maintain the sacred nature of the closest family secrets. They therefore never committed their thoughts, observations and skills to writing which would account for the scarcity of a written legacy. Just as language is a living entity deeply embedded in the culture, so tai chi has also evolved throughout the generations with close linguistic and cultural ties.

Language is an integral part of the expression of the culture whether in oral or written form. Culture in its many and various manifestations reflects the richness of the language. You cannot divorce the martial mind from the cultural mind. You need an understanding of the culture and the language in order to fully understand the martial arts of China. Once you have grasped these, all that remains is a lifetime's practice to attain your goals. In the Song of the Thirteen Postures in the Tai Chi Classics it states, "*Ru Men Yin Lu Xu Kou Shou, Gong Fu Wu Xi Fa Zi Xiu*" (入门引路须口授，功夫无息法自修) - To enter the door and be led along the road, you need oral instruction. Practise without ceasing, the way is through self-study.

LOOKING FOR THE MASTER WITHIN ONESELF

Fate and coincidence played a great part in my tai chi training in China. As it turned out, I began learning with a teacher, progressed to a sports coach and ended with a master. This was the order that my Chinese destiny mapped out for me. In hindsight, I sincerely believe it was the right order. Although each of them guided me a certain way along the path of my tai chi journey, eventually each of them released me to become the master of my own destiny and to find my own way.

I was like a child learning to ride a bicycle being steadied by the guiding hand of his father. Eventually the father lets go and, unbeknown to the child, he continues to ride unaided along the road. If he keeps facing forward, secure in the belief that his father's hand still has hold, then he will never fall off. But if he should doubt himself, look back over his shoulder, see his father in the distance and subsequently lose balance, then all is lost. Have faith in your teachers. Believe in their ability and more importantly believe in yourself.

"Searching" in the West seems to be very closely followed by "Finding". Ours is a society of immediacy. If we want something, we want it now. We are not prepared to wait, be patient, work hard and struggle in order to achieve. This philosophy also applies to tai chi. Hence our martial arts magazines are full of "How to do" books and tapes both from those who purport to be experts and masters to those who actually are masters. The appetite for consumption of Chinese martial arts in the West is so voracious that it seems impossible to saturate the market with these instructional devices. And everyone wants to learn from the outstanding teachers in their field. I am sure that I am not alone at feeling uneasy with this state of affairs. Having an impersonal relationship with the voice and image of a master at second hand is not my idea of learning. It must be on a personal face to face basis or not at all.

There are several traps that people are falling into here. Firstly, they believe that, if they train with the best teachers even by correspondence or the visual image, they too will in turn become the best. Secondly, they don't seem to think that it is necessary to leave the comfort of their own living rooms and the remote control facilities of their VCR's to become a martial arts expert. Thirdly, they do not see the necessity for building up one's skills progressively over a great number of years through daily practice and sheer hard work. No master ever acquired sublime skills without training at least five hours a day every day of his life, tolerating fatigue, pain, boredom, blood, sweat and tears. In Chinese there is a phrase *Chi Ku* (吃苦) which means to endure hardships and be capable of extreme hard work. In Chinese it literally means to eat bitterness. Without tasting bitterness you cannot hope to taste the sweetness of achieving a high level of ability. The two are simply incompatible and irreconcilable.

Nowadays it is relatively easy to train with the most outstanding Chinese masters. For their part they are busy touring America, Europe and Australia to promote the cherished arts that they hold so dear. On the one hand, this is a very positive trend. It is the duty of their inheritance to spread their art. On the other hand, it is negative because the student no longer has to find the master, beat a path to his door and through a display of patience and dedication plead to be accepted. No student is vetted for his suitability and acceptability. Provided he has the cash, that is the only criterion he has to meet. Now the master comes to him and the other students. The roles appear to have been reversed. Of course, this is a practical solution. Instead of the many individually seeking the few, the few can be flown in all expenses paid with a very attractive fee at the end of it. And why not? Tai chi is a desirable commodity. Why should those who possess its skills give them away cheaply when those in the West who only pretend to possess them sell them at extremely high prices? Why not let market forces take over? If you want the best, you have to pay for it. Just don't expect that you also will become the best, simply by being in the same seminar room with a great master for three hours. It takes a lot more *Chi Ku* than that. Equally, just because I have trained with some outstanding tai chi coaches and famous masters does not automatically make me outstanding and famous. It is not a question of <u>who</u> I have trained with but <u>how</u> I have trained myself. There is a Chinese saying "*Ming Shi Chu Gao Tu*" (名师出高徒) - Famous teachers can train outstanding disciples. However, this is not always the case. A good teacher does not necessarily produce good students. Of course it helps. It is a good student who produces a good student. The same applies to sons and fathers. Simply because my father is or was a famous master does not necessarily make me an equally famous master. Not all sons wish to follow in their fathers' footsteps. And if they do so only begrudgingly to continue the family tradition, then that tradition is inevitably weakened. It cannot be accepted unequivocally that the disciples or heirs of a famous master will necessarily possess the skills of their ancestors. What I would say is that being a model student, regardless of who your teacher is, gives you the potential for being a good and even an outstanding teacher.

To reinforce my belief that one's apprenticeship from student to teacher to master should be a gradual process, let me cite the example of my own master, Mei Ying Sheng. In the 1960's he began by learning and practising the simplified form of tai chi in his home town of Leshan in Sichuan Province. He was a doctor of medicine and acupuncturist who saw the practice of tai chi as a means of promoting the health of his patients. In the 1970's, he learned traditional Yang style from fifth generation masters who had studied under the fourth generation Master Li Chun Nian, an early disciple of Yang Cheng Fu. In the 1980's he studied with fourth generation Master Fu Zhong Wen in Shanghai and Gu Liu Xin. In 1983 Mei Ying Sheng was awarded the title of the outstanding martial arts instructor by the Chinese National Wushu Association. In 1993 he was made a member of the Council of the China Yongnian International Tai Chi Chuan Association, which is the governing body for traditional Yang style tai chi in China. Along the way he has published dozens of tai chi articles in mainland China, Taiwan, Hong Kong, Singapore, Europe and America and is a member of the editorial staff of the magazine "*Zhongguo Tajiquan*". Over the years he has taught more than 13,000 students, of whom the best have won medals in international competitions. He has attended many national and international tai chi conferences where he has won prizes or been given awards for his lifetime service to Chinese martial arts. He represents living proof of what achievements are possible if one is prepared to dedicate oneself to one's art and taste bitterness - *Chi Ku*.

The reality is that associating with greatness does not necessarily make one great. Training under a famous master for a day-long seminar, having one's photograph taken by his side, pushing hands with him for two minutes and sitting next to him at the dinner table are all wonderful memories and the source of inspiration, but they are all too fleeting and of no lasting substance. The real answer lies within oneself - one's attitude to learning, one's dedication to practice, and an overwhelming desire not only to emulate one's teacher but in the spirit of all humility even to surpass him.

CONCLUSION

Confucius said "*San Ren Xing, Bi You Wo Shi*" (三人行，必有我师). Among any three people walking, there must be my teacher. We should all have the humility to realize that we can learn from one another.

There are many erudite scholars in China including my own Master, Mei Ying Sheng, who can write more knowledgeably and eloquently about tai chi than I ever could. If I can make a small contribution towards making this priceless Chinese national treasure that is tai chi more accessible to western followers, towards bringing together Chinese masters, coaches and teachers in a greater appreciation and understanding of each other's work, then I shall have achieved much.

One never stops learning. Someone who is only one step ahead of you is worth learning from. In hindsight I made a natural progression in my choice of guides on the tai chi journey - from a humble teacher, through an advanced level sports coach to a traditional master. Fate played a hand in this sequence, coincidence too. In fact, fate seemed to play quite a significant part in my entire time in China. Fate chose well. If I had begun in the reverse order, I should not have learned a hundredth part of what I eventually learned. I was not prepared linguistically, culturally, mentally or physically at the beginning. The initial challenges and demands were great enough. Steadily I made a gradual progression up the ladder. I am still nowhere near the top, barely past the first rung. This does not discourage or dishearten me. The realization that there is still so much to learn and to accomplish fires me to continue and persevere with my tai chi journey in the quest for the supreme ultimate.

China is a country full of contradictions and paradoxes. There are probably contradictions within the pages of this book. I am aware of some if not all of them but I chose not to change any of them. The intention was not to present an incontrovertible account of what tai chi is or how it should be taught, learned and practised. Tai chi is like a language all of its own - a living, breathing, feeling entity which is constantly changing whilst staying reassuringly intrinsically the same. It simply appears different when viewed from different angles - just like the country of its origin.The map of China looks like a cock. If you look at it more closely, however, other images may begin to appear.

Wen Yi De San (问一得三) - Ask one question and get three answers. I originally went to China to look for the truth about tai chi, to get some ultimate answers. I simply ended up with more answers which in turn raised more questions than I had in the first place. The sum total of my quest for the supreme ultimate fighting art just left me with a better quality of questions than in the first place and inspired me to spend the rest of my life looking for some of the answers.

Shi Fu Ling Jin Men, Xiu Xing Zai Ge Ren (师傅领进门，修行在个人). After the teacher has led you inside the door, how well you practise is up to you as an individual.